M000215917

"Intriguing, intelligent and insightful, Judy Apps advocates an interconnected future in which we capture the strengths of both left and right
brain thinking. She shares her deep and magical understanding of one
of the biggest challenges of our times - getting people to connect at a
meaningful level with wisdom and wholeheartedness."
Kate Burton, coach and author of *Live Life. Love Work*
and *Coaching with NLP for Dummies*

"The authenticity of our relationships depends on our willingness
and ability to truly communicate and not only to converse. *The Art of
Communication* is a wise, compassionate and enormously helpful guide
in how to do so. Importantly, it also describes the reasons why, and the
ways in which we don't communicate. In offering clear and practical
support and encouragement to engage wholeheartedly with each other,
it is also extremely timely in these turbulent times. In needing to link up
together in real-ationships and as a global community, its message is
vital as to whether and how we survive and thrive as a species."
Dr. Jude Currivan, Cosmologist, author of *The Cosmic Hologram*
and co-founder of WholeWorld-View (www.wholeworld-view.org)

"I love this wonderful new book by Judy Apps. It really is the real thing
about the *art* of communication, in particular about the more elusive,
hard-to-describe *art* of communication, when something spontaneous,
meaningful and heartfelt happens between people in a conversation.

Sometimes when people communicate, some kind of intangible energy
connection seems to get sparked between them. When that happens people start to experience themselves as more present, and more seen and
more heard. Everyone starts somehow to feel more alive, awake and fully
human, blessed even. Something that matters changes, becomes more
soft and open, becomes more possible.

We love to experience these ordinary, not-ordinary, magical moments in
life when something new emerges and a new level of understanding is
there. There's a lovely spark, a connection, a felt sense of meaning and

expansion of being. We've touched each other in our deepest places of our shared humanity, and it's a joyful moment.

This deeper level of communication is usually so hard to describe. Judy Apps calls it 'the alternative world of real communication'. It's a paradox really, to learn how to be spontaneous in a skilful, warm-hearted and creative way. How do some people get to be naturally gifted at what we might think of as an intuitive ability?

In our fracturing, uncertain, dehumanising world many of us are quick to anger and alienation. Judy Apps' approach and the practical research, suggestions, examples and activities she offers in this book, offer a space to breathe and an opportunity to learn new ways.

It's a timely and important book for everyone who wants to help create a positive human future. It's a great resource for people who want to use their words to heal and not to hurt. It's a beautiful and inspiring manual on everyday communication and on how you can personally nurture and practice the core skillset of this intangible yet essential art.

It's an excellent and wise guidebook you'll want to absorb and be deeply informed by as you find your own way to the real, living heart of conversation."
Judith Lowe, Director at PPD Learning; Training and Coaching in Systemic and Generative NLP

"Such a communicator is Judy Apps that she's drawing us in one moment with a quote from Rumi, and the next with a line from Mariah Carey. In a book about deep authentic connection, Judy offers advice and insight about how to create moments of flow and magic in communication. For anyone who wants to have meaningful, insightful conversations that go beyond tricks and techniques, this is a powerful and wise book."
Sarah Smith, Director, Indigo Leadership

"Judy Apps has a gift for seeing how we are and has cleverly decon-structed how we relate to each other. She has given us a really helpful map for us to reach out to others and through simple conversations, satisfy our deep yearning to be more connected. She shows us the value of letting our real selves emerge, how we can do that, and more importantly that it is safe to do so."

Gina Lazenby, Best-selling author of Feng Shui titles, founder of the Healthy Home Retreat, radio show host and speaker on community gathering, wisdom and feminine leadership

"In our times when it's easy to feel separated, divided and overwhelmed, this book is unbelievably timely. Friendly, practical, wise and sometimes uncomfortably accurate, reading it is itself like having an intimate conversation. It clearly contains many years of personal and professional experience. I'll certainly be recommending it to colleagues and clients."

Neil Scotton, Co-Founder, The One Leadership Project

"Your life evolves one conversation at a time. Judy Apps has done a fabulous job of demonstrating this truth and how to access the power and potential that can exist within your next conversation."

Nick Williams, Leadership guide and author of sixteen books including *The Work We Were Born To Do*

"Great read! *The Art of Communication* will help you connect with your authentic self, challenge your thinking and eliminate negative self-talk that interferes with meaningful conversations. It helps you explore the role of your right brain in influencing the degree of presence we have in any conversations."

Gamiel Yafai, Diversity and Inclusion strategist and author of *Demystifying Diversity*

"A delightful book on a tricky topic which is handled deftly by the author. I particularly like the many anecdotes that illustrate so well the points being made to lead us to being better at meaningful conversations."

Paul Matthews, Author of *The L&D at Work Trilogy* and founder of People Alchemy

"If you want to improve the way you communicate, read this book. Judy Apps shows you how to trust your intuition, be spontaneous and let go of previously held beliefs and behaviours in order to create honest conversations that lead to positive outcomes."

Elizabeth Kuhnke, Executive Presence Coach, Author of *Body Language: Learn How to Read Others and Communicate with Confidence*

"I highly recommend this life enhancing book. It is insightful, thought provoking, encouraging, well written and fun to read. It made me believe in myself and feel eager to go out and practice the learning in my personal and professional life."

Celia Morris, MBA (Chartered) FCIPD, Training and Development Manager, Railways Division, Mott MacDonald

"A must-read book for left-brained technologists, accustomed to presenting facts and numbers, but who struggle to reach their audience (be it one person or a hundred) at a more personal level. Judy's guidance will give you the confidence to relax, draw on the right-hemisphere of your brain and teach you to enjoy interacting as human to human. It is full of gems that you will keep going back to, as you continue to improve your presentation and communication skills."

Graham Nixon, IT Partner, KPMG (ret'd), Commodore of the Royal Southern Yacht Club

THE ART OF COMMUNICATION

HOW TO BE AUTHENTIC, LEAD OTHERS AND CREATE STRONG CONNECTIONS

Judy Apps

CAPSTONE
A Wiley Brand

© 2019 Judy Apps

Registered office
John Wiley & Sons Ltd, The Atrium, Southern Gate, Chichester, West Sussex, PO19 8SQ,
United Kingdom

For details of our global editorial offices, for customer services and for information about how to apply for permission to reuse the copyright material in this book please see our website at www.wiley.com.

Wiley publishes in a variety of print and electronic formats and by print-on-demand. Some material included with standard print versions of this book may not be included in e-books or in print-on-demand. If this book refers to media such as a CD or DVD that is not included in the version you purchased, you may download this material at http://booksupport.wiley.com. For more information about Wiley products, visit www.wiley.com.

Designations used by companies to distinguish their products are often claimed as trademarks. All brand names and product names used in this book are trade names, service marks, trademarks or registered trademarks of their respective owners. The publisher is not associated with any product or vendor mentioned in this book.

Limit of Liability/Disclaimer of Warranty: While the publisher and author have used their best efforts in preparing this book, they make no representations or warranties with respect to the accuracy or completeness of the contents of this book and specifically disclaim any implied warranties of merchantability or fitness for a particular purpose. It is sold on the understanding that the publisher is not engaged in rendering professional services and neither the publisher nor the author shall be liable for damages arising herefrom. If professional advice or other expert assistance is required, the services of a competent professional should be sought.

Library of Congress Cataloging-in-Publication Data

Names: Apps, Judy, author.
Title: The art of communication : how to be authentic, lead others and create
   strong connections / Judy Apps.
Description: Chichester, West Sussex, United Kingdom : John Wiley & Sons,
   [2019] | Includes index. |
Identifiers: LCCN 2018058856 (print) | LCCN 2019001513 (ebook) | ISBN
   9780857088109 (Adobe PDF) | ISBN 9780857088048 (ePub) | ISBN 9780857088079
   (hardcover)
Subjects: LCSH: Interpersonal communication.
Classification: LCC BF637.C45 (ebook) | LCC BF637.C45 A686 2019 (print) | DDC
   153.6—dc23
LC record available at https://lccn.loc.gov/2018058856

Cover Design: Wiley

Set in 10/12.5pt RotisSansSerifStd by SPiGlobal, Chennai, India

Printed in Great Britain by TJ International Ltd, Padstow, Cornwall, UK

10 9 8 7 6 5 4 3 2

For John

CONTENTS

Intelligence is of two kinds ...
– Jalāl ad-Dīn Muhammad Rūmī, Persia, 1207–1273

We should take care not to make the intellect our god; it has, of course, powerful muscles, but no personality. It cannot lead, it can only serve; and it is not fastidious in its choice of a leader.
– Albert Einstein, born in Germany, 1879 –1955

It is not rational to assume, without evidence, that rationality can disclose everything about the world, just because it can disclose some things. Our intuition in favour of rationality, where we are inclined to use it, is just that – an intuition. Reason is founded in intuition and ends in intuition, like a pair of massive bookends.
– Iain McGilchrist, Britain, 1953 –

Part One

Introduction: Amazing Conversations

> *Happy the moment when we are sitting here, you and I,*
> *With two forms and with two figures but with one soul, you and I.*
> – Rumi

Some conversations give you a buzz of connection that surprises and delights. In such conversations time stands still and the boundaries between you collapse, allowing something new and exciting to emerge. But how can you encourage such connections to happen more often when conversation is by its nature spontaneous and unpredictable?

Prologue: Just Another Conversation

The little cabin we booked to rent in Shropshire was next door to an old house containing a restaurant that was shut at present. The owner, Elizabeth, came out to meet us and briefly explained that her husband wasn't available to open the restaurant during our stay as he was currently ill. She showed us around our cabin, invited us to contact her if we needed anything, and then withdrew. Later, as we strolled out to explore, we paused by display shelves in the front garden containing a variety of interesting jams and pickles and unusual garden plants for sale, set up by our host.

We didn't see Elizabeth again until the morning of our departure a few days later, when she emerged from the house to wish us goodbye. As we said our thanks and farewells, we quietly asked her about her husband, and she explained that after a few years of ups and downs with cancer, his condition was now terminal and the time remaining probably short. As we listened, she told us about his work as a restaurant chef, their life in other cities, and some of the challenges of running things on her own now. We admired her garden produce and plants and commented on the variety of birds that were attracted by the food she put out in feeders. Encouraged by our interest, she told us about her excitement a couple of days before, when in the early dawn she had witnessed five nuthatch fledglings leave the nest. Time was suspended for a few moments and I felt physically the frisson of our connection.

What was it? A short inconclusive conversation with a stranger. Yet I took much more from our conversation than some sad facts and some happier ones. It felt as if we had shared for a moment a larger theme of life. Such words are perhaps too abstract and fail to recognise how real the exchange felt – to each of us, I think. The truth lay in some in-between-ness; and it touched us.

What *Is* the Art of Communication?

I'm aware of so many oddities in communication. Why, for instance, did someone thank me for helping them make the best decision of their life on an occasion when I'd offered neither advice nor sympathetic words? And why did a friend come out with a form of words not even strictly connected with our conversation that unblocked a stuck feeling I'd had for a long time? Why did I feel a beautiful shiver of connection with someone during a conversation that superficially had merely been about the best time to visit Crete? And why did I get goose bumps in the silences between words in a conversation with someone?

Maybe you recognise that frisson of something shared? I have encountered it at different times in my life. Several years ago, on a course, chatting with a fellow participant for the first time, something about her words and attitude touched a chord so that I felt I had known her for a long time, and I went home buzzing with the energy of the encounter. I had the feeling sometimes also as a child, when my mother spoke to me about this and that at bedtime. I recall a tingling feeling of timeless pleasure and of not wanting the moment to end. There have been other times when someone has spoken to me of something personal to them and I've known that no response is needed, just my listening. What they are speaking about doesn't even have to be anything particular. It's sufficient that *they* are absorbed by it, and I am connected to them in their absorption, inside their space.

Frisson of Connection

Before we go further, recall for a moment times when you've felt a special connection when you communicated with someone.

- Remember a time when you had a conversation that felt especially enjoyable or remarkable. Maybe it felt more *real*, more three-dimensional somehow, than normal encounters? Or maybe an ordinary conversation miraculously lifted off to another plane and it was as if a veil had lifted between you? You felt a *thrill* of pleasure like waves of energy running all over your skin and you felt intensely alive.

- Spend a moment or two remembering the occasion and capture the feeling you had at the time.
- Ask yourself, what gave you pleasure? What made it exceptional? Accept whatever answers pop up in your mind.

In such conversations you are met in your soft centre, that beautiful, timeless part of you. From time to time, through such communion, where two people draw close, something creative is generated, some idea, some insight, some glimpse of new wisdom or truth.

You may find my opening story inconclusive, even trivial, and a long way from what you've understood about communication, particularly business communication. A common received view is that communication is about having opinions, knowing what you want and 'getting your message across'. But there's a huge gap between people hearing what you say, even appreciating aspects of it, and their connecting with you – let alone acting on what you say or changing their thinking or attitude because of it. Most talk – in meetings, the boardroom, presentations, conferences – doesn't cross that gap, however fluent your language, firm your voice and confident your physiology.

Clearly, conversation has unexplored depths that are not covered in simple manuals on small talk or conversational skills. For just as surely, my most productive conversations have been capable of breaking any of the usual 'rules of conversation', such as clarity of purpose, sharing of time, use of questions to elicit information, avoidance of silence, focus on meaning and so on. Those who inspire and kindle new thinking are doing something different – fundamentally different. Genuine communication is about crossing that gap.

We all struggle with communication at times. Do you sometimes find yourself in a situation where you'd like to say something but don't know what to say, or you know what you want to say but can't find the right opportunity to say it? Have you chatted to someone, wanting to connect with them, but realised you weren't really communicating with each other at all?

When you examine communication, you might be struck by the artificiality and sheer awkwardness of many interactions, even between people who are accomplished in the art of conversation. The truth is that many interactions are less than authentic, as people tend to operate from habitual positions largely beyond conscious awareness – to fit in, please people or avoid embarrassment, look knowledgeable, be admired or seize business advantage.

In the final chapters of my last book, *The Art of Conversation*, I began to explore some of the ways we can connect more deeply and fruitfully with each other. But communicating at that level doesn't naturally result from increased competence. We talk about communication as if it's a skill you can acquire step by step, and to an extent that is true: there is much you can learn that will make your conversations more fluent and satisfying. But there is the uncomfortable truth that, however much you may hone your skills as a communicator, no matter how interesting your facts, however fascinating your stories, even how well you share the conversation, deeper more meaningful communication does not naturally follow on from conversational competence. It requires something rather different.

The Risks of Spontaneity

The first and major challenge of conversation is that it's essentially a spontaneous activity, an everyday improvisation. At times we can prepare, but we can't safely predict when we're going to have a conversation or how it's going to pan out. In conversation – there's no getting away from it – we have to think and speak on the hoof.

For many people, speaking freely represents a risky enterprise. Not only might the other person take something the wrong way, but you might also say something you might regret, or embarrass yourself by talking garrulously or having absolutely nothing to say. Surrounded as we are by spin, sound bites, Twitter and Facebook, spontaneity can feel downright dangerous. Today, a trivial unconsidered remark can go viral in minutes, spiralling out of control in the glare of digital publicity. The actor Benedict Cumberbatch innocently used an outdated word to describe actors of colour and was pilloried for it. The novelist Hilary Mantel was hit with death threats after comparing the Duchess of Cambridge's situation to that of a 'shop window mannequin' in a thoroughly sympathetic article. Good reason to be cautious, you might think.

So, most people exert whatever control they can – ever more so in the current environment. Does such control work? It does, but only to a limited degree. Many recognise control for what it is and find it limited and tedious. Even leaving out 'fake news', there is a widespread mistrust of words, especially words spoken powerfully. We no longer believe the tightly scripted speech and want something less formulaic and more energising than the talk of repetitive politicians, un-nuanced interviewers, and relentlessly *jolly* media conversationalists.

POPULARITY OF THE UNPREDICTABLE

Among the public there is an appetite for more genuine communication that is partially fed by reality television programmes. Never has there been such curiosity to know the private lives and quirks of personalities in the media or to be a fly on the wall in the lives of ordinary people. It was surely this eagerness in the face of television's increasing predictability that spawned the rush of 'real life' programmes from the late 1990s onwards. *Big Brother, Strictly Come Dancing, The Apprentice, The Great British Bake Off, The X Factor, I'm a Celebrity, Love Island* and other programmes came along to feed our appetite for the unexpected, showing ordinary people or the semi-famous being challenged in various situations and often caught with their defences down. Admittedly, the footage is stage-managed for broadcast, but it still gives the audience many pleasurable intimate glimpses of unplanned moments.

Live shows offer the thrill of the unexpected and energise audiences with the anticipation of disaster. Fly-on-the-wall documentaries capture the misdemeanours and blunders of real life. Compilations of amateur clips of domestic disaster or embarrassment remain popular – the bride falls over, a child does a trick and comes to grief, people fall unsuspecting into water. Wildlife programme makers discovered the popularity of 'how it's done' behind-the-scenes filming, and include real-life difficulties and disasters encountered during the shooting.

The style of the 'reality' programme has leaked into politics too, and the politician who seems the most 'real' – or merely the most unpredictable – is often the one that catches the popular vote by feeding this compulsion to be surprised and shocked.

In popular entertainment, there's no comedian as popular as the one who risks spontaneity. Robin Williams, for example, had such a talent for improvising that for some parts of his films the script would read, 'Robin will do his stuff here'. Billy Connolly sounds surprised and delighted sometimes by his own adlibbing. It's such a winning style that other successful comedians such as Michael McIntire hone their tried and tested material to make it sound as if what they're about to say has just occurred to them that very minute.

Audiences love especially the unpredictability of comedians who can't resist laughing at their own gags. Dudley Moore and Peter Cooke often used to break down in laughter during their sketches to the delight of their audiences. You'll find at least half a million viewings on YouTube of the occasion when normally serious newsreader, Charlotte Green, got an impossible fit of the giggles while introducing an item about the first recording of a human voice. She even received a letter from Prince Charles thanking her for causing tears to roll down his cheeks.

STAKES TOO HIGH

Most of us love to watch the unpredictable on screen, but whatever the reason, when it comes to our own endeavours in real life the majority fall back on control. The stakes just feel too high.

Conversations That Aren't Real

I used to see an old work friend for a cup of tea and a chat every month or so. Gradually, I began to enjoy our meetings less, though I wasn't quite sure why. Was it when I became aware that she talked about everything except herself? Or was it when I noticed that her responses to whatever I asked had a generalised pleasantness that I found bland and boring? I began to want to say something outrageous to provoke a more extreme reaction, though I never did.

Then, months later, she informed me one day with some embarrassment that her wealthy husband had bought a luxury property elsewhere and was no longer living with her. Much later, she hinted that an acrimonious breakdown had been brewing for months. Feeling vulnerable, she'd been unable to talk about it. No wonder our conversations hadn't seemed real. I wished I had known at that time how to reach her.

When threatened – and I suppose my friend was afraid of exposure or just lacked the words to explain her situation – most people fall back on the predictable. We may be entertained at times by their conversation; we may be offered facts, conversation may flow; but none of that brings the conversation alive or gives either party satisfaction. In the absence of openness we miss genuine connection, the very qualities that make communication valuable and enjoyable.

In an age when many, especially in public life, have mastered the social skills for talking about anything and everything at the drop of a hat, it's easy to think that we've all become *too* good at it. Goodness, we hear enough conversations around us! But when all they do is follow stock procedures, the interchanges end up predictable or contrived and words lose their potency. It's not the way to more meaningful communication.

Secret of Whole-Mind Conversation

So how *do* we approach communication if not through control? From time to time you may meet someone who has the ability to say the perfect thing at the appropriate moment. They come up with original insights, spark connections that galvanise others, and offer words of comfort at the right time. Their communication opens people to each other in ways that seem miraculous. 'Talking to Loyd was like talking to myself, only more honest', says Codi of her friend and lover in Barbara Kingsolver's *Animal Dreams*. Their conversations may make the hairs at the back of your neck stand up or create a dopamine rush with their promise of future possibility. Some conversations have even changed history.

If you want some of this magic, then you have to look beyond conversational fluency and operate from a more intuitive place, radically different from the conscious or habitual intelligence normally employed in conversation. It's a place where *being* counts more than external skills, where treading lightly matters more than expertise, and where opening the heart is more important than critical evaluation. It's a step change. In this new world, few of the usual rules apply and success sits very close to failure. But the rewards when they come are rich.

The question is: how might you too call on this deeper intuition beyond conscious cleverness or accumulated knowledge when you interact with people? You have to be ready for the unpredictable and the unexpected. No amount of swotting to become more articulate, better at debate or more informed, no accumulation of funds of better stories, or even a more friendly manner or persuasive voice is going to grant you success. You have to be prepared for a kind of learning that's surprising, that will show you yourself in the raw, question your relationships with others, and focus on being rather than doing.

As a first step, you have to contemplate a loosening of attachment to preconceptions, step by step progress towards conclusions, and excessive future and past thinking. Just as the mathematics student suddenly discovers that advanced maths has as much to do with intuition as calculation, so the advanced communicator discovers that success depends as much on inner shifts and warmth of heart as on rational intelligence and social competence.

The rational conscious mind, which mostly utilises the left hemisphere of the brain, tends to proceed from step to step with focused attention to detail. But deeper communication makes creative use of the more holistic right-brain, with its sustained, wide-angled alertness that can process information all of a piece without conscious focus on component parts. It's prompted by the immediate and doesn't fall back on well-worn wisdom and knowledge. And it tends to do this quickly, much faster than conscious thought. Using your whole mind, left- and right-brain, enables you to trust your intuition and creativity and brings you closer to people. Fresh discoveries about the roles of the different hemispheres of the brain enable us to understand the underlying science for the first time.

In this book we're going to look at the characteristics of this deeper conversation as well as certain traits that masquerade as such. You'll discover how to make greater use of your deeper intelligent mind, a mind that is far more intuitive and creative than you could imagine.

Part Two

Opting for Control

> *We are like bowls on the surface of the water.*
> *The direction a bowl moves*
> *is controlled*
> *not by the bowl, but by the water.*
> – Rumi

There's always a tendency to control communication to avoid unwelcome surprises. Most people steer their conversation with habitual instructions to the brain, and these affect everything they say, mostly beyond self-awareness. With such agendas in place, stemming mainly from fear, they fail to truly show up when they encounter other people.

Control Rules

The first step toward more authentic communication is to look at control. There's a strong instinct to control our environment and plan what to say and how to say it. Control is pervasive and entrenched in our culture, the all-favoured modus operandi in politics, leadership, management, and every aspect of our lives. Much conversation today, whether social discourse, political interview, or media chat, *is* in fact highly measured and predictable.

Unsurprising, as we've seen, when social media lurks ever ready to spread a thoughtless comment globally and create havoc.

Some protect themselves by sticking blandly in 'social mode'. They articulate 'correct' social responses, stay within strict boundaries, and parrot received opinions while revealing nothing significant about themselves. Some act like machines and speak entirely without emotion. Others play games of charm and other manipulation, pretend insouciance or respond in a particular 'personality' or role.

At the same time, many are inhibited by self-consciousness, lack of self-esteem, fear, and other over-riding emotions. They guard their words, hide their feelings, and prepare in meticulous detail for significant occasions such as interviews, speeches and presentations. In the workplace every effort is made to avoid surprises; people are analysed and assessed; human traits are measured and evaluated – everything possible is done to create certainty and guarantee expected results.

Much has been written and spoken about how to maintain better control of events and people. Gradually, we have devised procedures that minimise surprise so that we know what to do for almost every eventuality. We find control everywhere, even *disguised* as freedom and spontaneity. Some people, especially in public life, play the role of spontaneity with an easy uncon-strained manner that disguises hard-headed calculation beneath the surface. General bonhomie can act as a strong self-defence, never allowing the real person to emerge and making anything but superficial connection unlikely. Most common of all is the tendency to speak with a filter permanently in place controlling what is said – for example, conversation with the aim of showing oneself in a good light, winning points, obtaining personal advantage, or pleasing people. The conversation can appear relaxed, but the impression is skin-deep. Some powerful populist politicians come into this category.

Control shows up too as habits of conversation that we are no longer capable of noticing in ourselves. Maybe we are negative and complain a lot or have the tendency to blame others. Maybe we display constant facile positivity in the face of good sense. Perhaps we instinctively say no to everything and miss opportunities. Such behaviours become our defaults, and they prevent us from living our desires or even asking ourselves whether we have desires at all. This can prevent anything new from surfacing in our lives. And it can get in the way of connection with other people.

WHAT IS CONTROL?

What does control consist of? In the simplest terms it's left-brain thinking, where rationality with its linear processes, coherent systems and concepts is promoted, while emotion and intuition are consigned to minor roles. With control, decisions are taken consciously, using the evaluating, analysing parts of the brain. Evidence is accumulated, examined and dissected. The method concentrates on building up 'facts' and getting the details right, then abstracting and categorising.

We have arrived at a point in history where the left-brain rules in business, politics, and public life; and, indeed, in every sphere of our lives we operate by more and more rules and increasing surveillance, accompanied by assurances that it's for our safety and general wellbeing. But we're missing out. There is a sense that the freedom and wonder of life is getting lost, and that it's not a small loss, but is changing us as human beings into something less attractive, less adaptable, and less inventive and creative.

Control certainly rules in the realm of communication. Reflect on how seldom – with a very few notable exceptions – public statements today surprise us. Spin and sound bites threaten to drown out debate. Much talking on radio and television – even the news – is delivered by means of adversarial interviews, micro-managed in tight time slots by producers, while politicians and business leaders play the game of 'answering' questions with prepared slogans to ensure predictable outcomes.

Well-versed politicians, scripted interviews, party lines, stock answers and stock emotions have become the common currency. Switch on the television and all too often you are greeted by an over-energetic smiling and laughing face that neither energises nor projects happiness, or a bland face that reacts to neither charm nor insult – it's make believe, robotic even, 'a mask of Plasticine smugness' as Russell Brand once referred to the expression of a typical politician. There are notable exceptions, but as we shall see, control agendas play a big part here too.

Being Thoroughly Prepared

Going through my father's possessions after he died, I discovered a tightly folded piece of paper in the inside pocket of his old dinner jacket, containing minutely written instructions for the execution of various dance moves. The waltz, quickstep, foxtrot, samba, and tango were all included. He came prepared! Yet, when did he imagine he might do his final swotting by tucking this information into a pocket of his dinner jacket? On a quick visit to the bathroom before asking someone to dance?

Many people approach conversation in the spirit of being thoroughly prepared, pinning their confidence on studied subjects of conversation and planned lines of enquiry. A man who had reached the top of his profession told me once, to my surprise, that he often prepared conversational topics before meeting people so that he wouldn't be left hanging without something topical or interesting to say.

Control has a lot going for it. You avoid unwelcome surprises and the unpleasant chaotic feeling that you're no longer master of yourself. Life constantly demands an instant response. A tiger wanders up to our cave – Hide? Run? Attack? Freeze? Quick – choose! An employee is underperforming. Talk to him? Show him a new way? Sack him? Decisions, decisions! We don't feel quick enough on our feet; it's so much more comfortable to have a ready answer. But does it work in conversation?

CONVENTIONAL CONVERSATIONAL SKILLS

The instinct to control responses in conversation is usually based on the good intention of responding well, but with control we never get beyond a general competence in communication – the deeper possibilities of conversation just don't happen.

Most coaching in the art of conversation follows the control method. If you doubt your conversational skills and seek help from experts or books, you will probably be assisted to become more articulate. You'll work at your use of language, and study to get accent and inflection right. You'll practise to make your sentences flow, and you'll learn anecdotes to have ready to call upon. You'll buff up your opinions and hone your arguments; you'll become skilful in the arts of oratory and debate and also in small talk with its polite balance of question and answer. You'll learn how to put expression into your voice so that you sound interested – spontaneous even.

Learned Spontaneity

Even such a practised and fluent communicator as Sir Winston Churchill used to spend enormous time and effort practising and learning to *sound* spontaneous in his public speeches. His great friend F. E. Smith jibed that Winston spent the best years of his life preparing *impromptu* remarks.

CALCULATION

More of us than would admit to it go into conversation at least some of the time with a calculation. It may be a simple aim to look good, to win points, or to be liked. These calculations are sometimes conscious, but often they are largely invisible to us – default responses that direct the tone and direction of the interaction. It's so normal that few of us notice that defaults are operating. But as we don't fully show up when such filters are in operation, the result is lack of connection. Desire to control conversation to feel more secure turns out to be the very factor that prevents us from truly connecting with people.

Whenever human being speaks with human being wonderful things can happen – but only if both parties are fully present. If one or both are in 'default' mode, nothing new or interesting emerges.

We are all used to showing each other only a fraction of our interior world. Depending on whom we're talking to, we've learned to hide the parts of ourselves that might be seen as weak or needy, angry or unattractive. So, to avoid experiences that have in the past brought us rejection or loneliness and to gain love and acceptance from others, we edit ourselves little by little. Laughter is one of the whips that keep us in line. To avoid unwelcome laughter, we suppress our spontaneity and originality – even our humour and creativity – and learn to appear 'ordinary' (or for some, 'special' within strictly understood parameters). With such strategies, we no longer respond spontaneously to others and thus diminish ourselves, becoming smaller, less authentic versions of who we really are.

Control Agendas

If you want to excel at the art of conversation beyond mere facility with words, it's helpful to recognise your own agendas. We don't tend to notice them because they are habitual and finally become automatic. Many things we say to each other are meaningless, but to us are perfectly normal. We just don't realise that our way of speaking to each other, familiar as it is, is a choice, because it's our usual medium, the water we swim in.

Certain situations trigger particular thoughts, which create the same response from us, day after day. These vary from person to person, but for each of us change remarkably little over time. Basically, they are simple instructions to the brain for different circumstances that guide what we say and how we say it. They are usually driven originally by inner gremlins of 'musts' and 'shoulds', such as, 'I've got to look good here', or 'I need to impress my boss at this point', or 'Danger! I must hide this'. The instructions we use most become habits, and eventually become buried in the unconscious and invisible to our conscious selves – though still a burden: we should-er our shoulds heavily!

At our house, we have a newly installed three-way tap in the garden. You turn a switch one way and water from the tap is directed into the garden hose; switch it another way and the water comes through a short length of tube to fill the watering can; a third position produces water straight from the tap. Many of us approach conversation in the same way by automatically switching on the appropriate tap. In a social situation we adopt a charming and friendly stance; in a work situation we may adopt the business tone of our professional role. It works pretty well. We are accustomed to such adaptation and even expect it in deference to 'politeness' or social convention. It can be seriously disconcerting when someone breaks the code instead of 'playing the game'.

The filters we have in place lead us to say certain things and refrain from others, setting patterns for conversation. These patterns become so ingrained that they govern much of our behaviour. With some people it's like singing to a single tune, with a title such as 'Win at All Costs', 'Complain and Blame', or 'Defend My Reputation', which they play again and again. Others act out the typical human responses of fight, flight, or freeze by becoming a conversational bully, scaredy-cat, or corpse.

Habitual responses are quite lazy. We see what we expect and react accordingly. For example, we may have labelled a certain friend irresponsible, and he only has to say he's decided to take a day off work for us to jump to our automatic conclusion and think 'irresponsible!'

The biggest weakness of the process of filtering is the impossibility of real connection with the other person. Agendas in all their various guises bring tension into breathing, posture, and body language and create a barrier. However much you may be fulfilling your agenda, you are not genuinely present to the other person. Yet, selfish or well-intentioned, agenda-driven reactions become accepted as regular communication in our minds, even as they skew responses and cause the real rewards – such as connection, creative thinking, and combined intelligence – to be lost.

They come in various guises.

1. LOOKING GOOD

The desire to look good often highjacks a conversation. Like many agendas, it involves subterfuge and disguise. People who are most successful at hiding may even seem open and available, while their real persona is safely protected and tucked away out of sight.

We all adopt masks at times. Feelings are catching and we don't want to burden others with our negative states, so we sometimes smile when we are sad and put aside our wounds at times when sharing them with others won't serve them or us. But we need to know we are doing it; we need to be conscious of it.

'Playing by the Rules' in Social Discourse

Instruction: Be nice! Say what people want to hear! Obey social convention!

Quite a lot of conversation is talking for talking's sake – gossiping, moaning, socialising to be seen, collecting people like trophies, merely doing what is expected in a situation. We conform to society's conventions that allow us to hide behind the polite formalities and empty routines of small talk. For many, there's a constant fear of transgressing the codes of communication of their particular circle. Some groups engage with each other with strict formality, others engage in robust debate or competitive repartee, but the most common default is being nice. You become a member of the group by following the group norm.

Being 'nice', we say what we think others want to hear. We reiterate empty phrases: 'And how was your holiday? Oh, that must have been exciting (in a non-excited voice). And what's Bill doing now?' That's fine at the beginning of a conversation but arid as a destination. That empty brightness of voice and erect posture reveal to any perceptive observer that you're not communicating at all, rather *avoiding* real communication by putting up a front of politeness. Even when smoothly managed, it brings formality to social situations, and unless transcended increases the distance between you.

Kate Chopin describes the process in her late-nineteenth-century novel, *Awakening*. The art of conversation, she says, at least for a woman, is to say nothing, just look appropriately pleased or sorry or indignant and always interested and entertained. And amazingly, the man will speak of you as entertaining and intelligent when you have said little more than, 'What do you do?' Isn't it great that women are no longer like that, we say – and then pause to wonder whether that is true.

A Carefully Planned Spontaneous Speech

 The desire to be appropriate and look good can be wondrously subtle. Tim Parks, an author who's pretty self-aware, gives a painfully honest and humorous personal example of how we like to come across as spontaneous even when we're deviously planning. He describes how, the moment he heard the news that he was on the shortlist for the Booker Prize for Fiction, he started to plan a modest acceptance speech in case he won. He ran over and over it in his mind, each time with new additions and flourishes. The speech would be clever, ironic, impressive, but above all modest, so that people would think what a nice ordinary guy he was to downplay his clearly brilliant mind: doubly modest in fact when compared to the subtle brilliance yet unpretentiousness of his speech. Many of us might squirm at the familiarity of his scenario.

Acting a Professional or Expert Role

Instruction: Look the part! Sound business-like! Maintain the status of your title!

If you want to hide in plain sight, there's nothing more straightforward than to use your work role as a mask. You stand straighter and stiffer than other people and use the abstract lexicon of business-speak to sound more masterful. You may devote much energy to projecting an image of 'infallibility'. The mask is impenetrable, never affording a glimpse of more vulnerable human emotions, such as sadness or disappointment. It successfully keeps others in the organisation at a distance.

Android Boss

 Laura worked in a dynamic young company with a young owner, and the company's success depended on new work coming in regularly. Laura found her boss very difficult to work with, but not because he was particularly unpleasant. The problem was that he gave nothing away. When she did a particularly good piece of work, she heard nothing from him. When things were clearly not going well with a particular account, everything was shrouded in secrecy and people felt unsupported. The word around the office was that the owner was an android, a machine, hopeless at human relationships. The tight control and lack of emotional connection diminished trust and affected morale.

Often, both participants in a communication are playing roles. In a business environment, conversations often take place between title and title. One senior manager I coached said he didn't want to know anything about the people who worked for him and certainly didn't want them to know anything about him; he found such information completely irrelevant. Communication for him was between boss and employee and followed set patterns of limited scope. Despite perennial talk of equality, much in the work sphere emphasises hierarchy by maintaining a particular kind of work-speak that simplifies relationships and distances people from each other.

Such simplification, though appearing to maintain control, can have serious downsides. Without genuine communication, much that is important for a business passes people by or fails to happen, and the failures can be catastrophic.

Deference Kills

 In his book *Outliers*, Malcolm Gladwell describes a famous Korean aeroplane crash in the 1990s. The pilot made a serious error in bad weather, and the younger co-pilot noticed the error but was so entirely stuck in the role of subordinate who doesn't question his superiors that he didn't like to point it out. The consequences were fatal. Their business culture emphasised the hierarchy of roles to such an extent that he didn't know how to communicate in any other way, *even when lives were at stake.*

Time and again in business and politics, people find themselves in the role of courtiers admiring the Emperor's new clothes – making comments with a verve and energy they do not feel or acting impassively while feeling strong emotion. To use ambiguous language is exhausting – it's a kind of lying and lying always saps energy. Maintaining your position, reputation, credit, or standing is exhausting too.

Many politicians, business leaders, and media personalities identify so completely with their role that we would be hard-pressed to separate the person from the role. For them, the process of listening is merely an opportunity to prepare their own next sally.

Living the Role Too Well

 The television programme *Dead Ringers* used to include an impression of former UK Prime Minister Tony Blair acting his role. In the sketch, he is so concerned with his image that he forgets what he is communicating and fails to stop when he reaches the stage directions on the autocue: 'Hello, I'm Tony Blair (reassuring gesture, concerned brow, smug smile).' This joke was so successful with audiences that it became a running gag on the show: 'Serious forehead, receding ears, why-does-nobody-love-me-any-more hand gesture. Compassionate Paul Smith suit. Sweaty teeth.'

Defending Self-Image

Instruction: Beware – danger! Protect yourself! Pull up the drawbridge!

When you defend your self-image to look good, other people's first impression of you may be of confidence and openness, but gradually other characteristics become evident. You seem confident, yes, but you never risk vulnerability. You may be full of opinions, but you don't express personal emotions. You may miss someone's impromptu injection of humour while you're busy defending yourself. You promote yourself and put your energy into making sure the cracks don't show. Your eternal vigilance destroys your ability to be spontaneous even as you act with confident ease and geniality.

The cracks show when, in your instinct to defend, you make knee-jerk responses, programmed by how you've reacted in the past. Someone fires at you, 'You're too sensitive', and you respond in the instant, 'No, I'm not!' Or someone accuses you of being too frightened to volunteer for a bungee jump and you retort, 'Don't be ridiculous!' There is no inner dialogue with the self in such responses. Some person or event presses your trigger and your gun goes off with no micro-space for choice.

When you try to protect yourself through self-defence, power struggles ensue, creating further necessity to defend and control. So, control, like any rigid defence, brings about what it's aiming to prevent.

One kind of defence that hides itself well is curiosity. Not a bad thing in itself, indeed an interest in the other person is crucial for good conversation, but some communicators use it as a screen to hide behind. They ask question after question, but reply to questions asked of them with phrases that hold others at a distance from their own affairs, thus keeping the ball constantly in the other person's court.

2. COMPETING TO WIN

Many, many are the 'I'm better than you' defaults. Listen to the masters of this genre, and you'll notice that they never pass up the opportunity in conversation to win a point and come out on top.

Some want to come across as cleverer than others. For some, it's their eye to the main chance: everything they hear translates to dollar signs, 'How can I profit here?' or 'Where's the advantage for me in this?' Some want to be the most successful; others want to emerge as the most powerful. Some want to be the most dramatic – even the most tragic or long-suffering if it's a way to achieve drama. Some succeed in having the last word in banter. Some merely want to be centre stage, to be the most important or get the most airtime. Others are interested in status. Some – and certain politicians spring to mind – sell themselves without pause, without a care for truth or good sense as long as they dominate the scene.

COUNTER-INTUITION

Your self actually grows and expands when not obsessed with itself.

Winning Profit or Power

Instruction: Find the advantage! Get the best deal! Come out on top!

This is the salesman's default. At its worst, it won't matter how many lies you tell, so long as the prize is won. If this filter motivates you, you won't have shame – it's the winning that counts. You have a powerful instinct to tell people what they want to hear, so that they'll buy what you have to offer. This may apply to car sales or to your personal image. So long as they buy it, anything goes. You'll recognise examples of this agenda in politics as well as in the salesroom.

Winning the Argument

Instruction: Win the point! Defend my viewpoint at all costs! Prove that I'm the cleverest!

You want to come across as the most knowledgeable or the most erudite. Every conversation is a debate, and debates are to be won. This style of conversation doesn't mind difference or even conflict – everything the other person says is an opportunity for you to reload your own argument and fire. You make points that reveal your superior knowledge or learning, and resist flexibility or compromise. Indeed, though you can express opinions forcefully, any convincing counter-argument feels like a personal attack on your sense of self.

Such desire to win may make you leap in early in a conversation to state your business in case you run out of time. People who are highly competitive usually hold a belief in scarcity. They think that there is not enough to go around and that they need to fight to be first to get at the prizes. With this belief, other people including friends can only ever be rivals.

Surpassing in Status/Comparing

Instruction: Look superior to the other person! Dominate the conversation! Obtain deference!

You want to look superior at all costs, and this might involve name-dropping and hinting at powerful connections. It gives you a distorted view, as everything is judged on its usefulness to your self-promotion and advancement. Your friends and lovers have to be beautiful to shine positively on you as their friend; contacts are dropped if they are not going to advance your interests; house, car, and hobbies have to promote your image. Your eye is always on personal advancement; you look out for deference.

If someone else tells an anecdote, you make sure you have an anecdote to cap it, even if it's a story of disaster. Okay, so they ran into a storm on a sailing holiday and had a hard time getting back into harbour? Big deal. *Your* boat was scuppered on the rocks and you were airlifted to safety at a cost of 100 000 dollars!

Conquering with Charisma

Instruction: Woo with expansive friendliness! Make people laugh! All eyes on me!

You can be highly defended and yet seem the opposite. You may project an image of natural spontaneity and be everyone's friend with a generalised affability. You may act the joker and seem happy-go-lucky even, but behind the scenes you're calculating the effect. Such fake spontaneity, including buffoonery and a happy-go-lucky image, is very common in public life today. There are Teflon politicians who create a charismatic public image, yet maintain a calculating eye on personal advancement, always working in their own self-interest.

Such behaviour may convince for a while, but that warm voice is actually no more open than the friendly-sounding electronic voice at the supermarket till informing you where to put your shopping bag. Your charisma never really invites people in; your friendliness never really connects with individuals, even as it beckons them to believe the image. Author and coach Tim Gallwey talks about the acts people have to make us believe they are wonderful, that are covering their actual wonderfulness. It's hard to relate to an act.

3. PLEASING AND APPEASING

It may seem strange to think of pleasing people as an agenda, but for many people keeping other people happy or on-side takes precedence over all else to such an extent that they are incapable of acting differently, *even when they are aware that it annoys others.* Sometimes, it presents itself as a kind of superior moral unselfishness. But as a default behaviour it stops people from thinking independently, encourages clinging and insincerity, and seldom promotes good relationships.

Pleasing People/Needing to be Liked

Instruction: Make people love me! Look happy! Everything is entirely okay!

A strong desire to please drives much of human behaviour, with its constant subtle undertones: 'Will this make people like me?', 'How will this come across?', or 'Might this upset someone?'

How impossible it is to say no to something when you cannot bear the slightest possibility of making someone unhappy! How difficult to speak your truth when you fear that others won't agree with you! Yet your voice and body language contradict you when you appease and placate. Someone asks, 'Would you like to come to the party?' And you reply, 'Er,' – slight stutter – 'er, yes, I'd ... love to ...' – voice tailing off.

The desire to please leads you to second-guess what the other person would like to hear, and then seek to provide it. Fear of getting it wrong or being rejected or coming across as selfish or aggressive or inadequate make it almost impossible to get it right and can be tiresome for other people.

You feel that you must be cheerful and positive at all times. 'How are you?', they ask. 'Oh, I'm fine', you reply with a little rise in pitch at the end of the phrase. This kind of pretence for others' benefit is another way of creating a barrier between you and the other person in conversation.

Not Rocking the Boat

Instruction: Don't threaten the status quo! Don't risk things getting worse! Yes, dear!

A particularly deadly form of pleasing is the default of not rocking the boat. Experience has perhaps taught you that opposition makes things worse, so you tread constantly on eggshells, avoiding conflict, never making a fuss. You try always to be the person that other people expect you to be. But you are not really present in any conversation; you are constantly wary – mild and acquiescent on the surface, but only as an act. Your responses are all fear-based, aiming hopelessly to keep the peace.

Put Others First

Instruction: Put others first at all times! Sacrifice! Self-immolate!

Agendas do not necessarily have their roots in selfishness: you may, for instance, feel that you always have to care for others before yourself or be generous as a principle. But when positive traits become fixed habits or compulsions, you are no longer free to respond in the most useful or creative way to people and circumstances.

Then you oppress others in your insistence. Someone once said to me of a mutual friend who had caring as a default: 'She has to feel sorry for me all the time – it's so exhausting!' If you have this default, other people are aware to a certain extent that you 'have to' behave in this way, and don't react with appropriate gratitude to the 'gifts' that you offer. Your self-sacrificing attitude feels like a burden on them.

In any case, compulsive goodness often hides non-expressed anger and resentment, which is picked up subconsciously by others and prevents close relationships.

4. PRESUPPOSITION AGENDAS

Numerous other agendas are based on your beliefs, and profoundly affect your ability to respond in a real way to others because they create instant knee-jerk reactions in you. True awareness doesn't know what it'll find. Agendas masquerading as beliefs instantly put the other person in a box.

Examples of this kind of filter might be:

- 'Success requires hard work'
- 'Marriage is sacrosanct'
- 'I must be perfect'
- 'Being late signifies disrespect'
- 'People aren't generally to be trusted'.

The Root Cause of Agendas is Fear

What drives these agendas? There's a compulsion – a familiar feeling of necessity. An inner voice urges, 'you must', 'you've *got* to', or 'you can't not', sometimes with the implied postscript, 'or else …'.

Behind the compulsion lies one root block: fear.

Looking good, social convention, professional role playing, self-defending, winning points, establishing status, charming, pleasing, putting others first – these responses are all attempts at control, at satisfying the gremlins of 'got to' and 'can't not'. And, through continued use, these blocks and attempts to control gradually sap our vitality and silt up the fountain of energy inside us.

This process takes place on an individual level and on a systemic level. Whole organisations run exhausting agendas – hidden myths to do with competition, perfection, or the impossibility of mistakes, kept in place by fear – and in truth such cultures are debilitating for employees and inimical to creative thought and connection.

On an individual level, each of us is scared of what might happen if we allow our vitality free rein. I might make a mistake or come across wrong, I might make a fool of myself, I might not be good enough, I might not be acceptable, or I might be discovered to be a fake. And so we cement into habit ways of behaving that started out as over-concern about our communication with other people and an intense need to be in control. We might like to think that emotion has nothing to do with it, but we're afraid of what others think – and they probably feel the same about us – so we fail to hear what pops up inside us to say and creep around the truth because we think we don't know how to say it.

Fear surfaces in various forms.

SELF-CONSCIOUSNESS

Worry about how you might be perceived turns your attention and energy inwards. Instead of thinking or doing or being, you think *about* thinking, doing, or being. You start to evaluate your performance even as you live it, stripping any enjoyment from it.

As you search your brain to find the right thing to say or the right question to ask, at some level you're aware of yourself in action, so you are no longer present. Fear of saying the wrong thing even makes you say the wrong thing. Thus, even as you create something, you tear it apart and consume it like a snake swallowing its own tail or like a car driver accelerating with one foot firmly on the brake.

Thinking About

 Coach Tim Gallwey asked his tennis opponent how he achieved a particularly good shot. The moment the man started to think *about* it and tried to analyse what he was doing, he became self-conscious and his game fell to pieces. One way to beat your opponent!

TRYING TOO HARD

Fearing failure, people try too hard and become tense. This is quite easy to spot in others, harder to realise when you're doing it yourself. You can notice it in people's language, which becomes convoluted and clunky, practically ensuring that they don't get what they want. 'I suppose you couldn't get me a copy of that report, could you?' 'I couldn't ask you a favour, could I?' The negative forms just cry out for the answer no.

A common effect of trying too hard is tediousness. Speakers attempt to include everything, and this striving kills any spontaneity or possibility of intuition and creativity, let alone connection with those they're speaking to. Concentrating on getting everything right, they forget *why* they're trying to get it right. When you strive in conversation, you set yourself apart from who you really are, and it's impossible for others to reach you in any meaningful way.

All that compulsion to look and sound competent, the striving to look impressive, the effort to win points, makes people clumsy with their interjections and not balanced enough to follow a conversation in its flow so that it can develop naturally. Comments often jar, efforts to hide effort feel uncomfortable, and everything conspires to create a vicious circle where they work ever harder and make things difficult for themselves.

One form of trying too hard is a striving for superiority. You walk into a room convincing yourself that you're better than everyone, misunderstanding that real confidence is to walk into a room without having to compare yourself with anyone at all.

INNER CONFLICT

When you become fearful, you attempt to hide parts of yourself that you feel are not acceptable and present yourself as something you are not. All this effort represents a huge and pointless drain on your energy.

You may recognise the paralysis that freezes you when there's an internal struggle inside you; for example, when your desire to move forward in one direction is matched by an equal and opposite fear of losing out if you do. Maybe you want to win something from someone but at the same time want them to see you as non-competitive. Or you want to be open and honest while wanting to hide big chunks of yourself at the same time. There are few things as exhausting as being pulled in different directions at once. It's also difficult for people interacting with you as they experience awkwardness or confusion.

STRESS AND PHYSICAL TENSION

Every kind of fear-based control introduces stress into the system and blocks you. Authenticity and spontaneity are sacrificed. Others detect in you something artificial and even untruthful. You cease to be quick on your feet and fall back on stock observations and responses. Struggling internally, the body loses some of its aliveness. You lose your natural flow and become tight. This happens particularly when you suppress emotions or pretend different emotions. The psychoanalyst Wilhelm Reich described this muscular defence we create against emotions we do not want to feel as 'body armour'.

Control will never lead to conversations that are organic and satisfying. Its checks and balances are crude compared to whole-mind thinking. We need a more intuitive approach.

Part Three

The Alternative World of Real Communication

> *You gather up your robes around you*
> *lest the water should wet them;*
> *You must dive down*
> *a thousand times deeper into the sea.*
> – Rumi

Introducing the 'new way'. Instead of aiming to 'manage' your conversations, you become willing to go with the flow. You discover how to use your whole mind, not just the rationality of the well-exercised left-brain but also the more diffuse and often-neglected wisdom of the right-brain. Your conversation moves away from reliance on habit into a different and subtler realm.

The *Je Ne Sais Quoi* of Communication

Communication is quite complex. There are the basics – your voice, posture, body language and fluency. There's language – your vocabulary, grasp of grammar and syntax. There's content – your ideas, stories, cognitive abilities and intellect. There's rapport – mirroring, tuning in to voice tone, facial expression and gesture. There's emotional intelligence – catching subtleties, understanding nuances of tone and appreciating atmosphere. Finally, there's the *je ne sais quoi* of communication, indefinable, elusive, hard-to-measure intuition that dances in the unpredictable moment.

In fact, many elements of advanced communication are indefinable, elusive and hard to measure. Yet, human beings take confidence from measuring. Communication skills training, for instance, often provides correction that can be accurately assessed and measured. If you fidget with your hands, you're told to hold them at your sides. If you lean informally to one side, you're told to stand vertical and balanced. If you look into space, you're told to use eye contact. The trouble is that while your energy and focus go on correcting what's wrong, you always remain slightly self-conscious, never quite able to dance spontaneously in the moment.

There's a whole world of difference between communicating effectively – a skill – and communicating profoundly with inner intelligence, intuition, qualities of mind, and psychology; and the difference is art not science. If you listen to any of the great international musical competitions, such as *Cardiff Singer of the World* or the *Tchaikovsky International Music Competition*, in which every finalist is brilliantly accomplished technically, the panel of judges invariably chooses the winner on something beyond technique: their exceptional ability to communicate something special – that *je ne sais quoi* – to their audience.

Moving to the next level in conversation requires you to make more use of your right-brain, to discover this *je ne sais quoi*. Wholeheartedness, staying open and present, paying exquisite attention, using your intuition, being spontaneous and creative, tapping into a silent well of wisdom within – these are all part of it. With these attributes, self-consciousness melts away and a huge well of energy is released, involving not just the mind, but also the heart, body, and spirit.

We use different parts of the brain for these different abilities, and that is where we'll go next.

1

USE BOTH HEMISPHERES OF THE BRAIN

> *Your heart knows*
> *that to seek book-learning and traditional knowledge*
> *when inspiration is at hand*
> *is like washing yourself with sand*
> *instead of water.*
> – Rumi

The different qualities of attention of the two separate hemispheres of the brain are highly relevant to different kinds of conversation. Neuroscientific advances of the past 50 years have greatly enriched our knowledge in this area.

Different Ways of Viewing Life

In the past, doctors did experiments on *dead* bodies and made inferences about the inner workings of *live* human beings. Then they studied activity in a living brain and claimed to discover immutable brain functions of the human being studied. Now they study the ability of synapses in the brain to reform and develop in order to find out about man's potential.

Our *way of observing* the world determines what we see and find out, and what we see and find out becomes our experience of the world that we observe. That is why *how* we attend to the world is crucial for our communication with each other, and why I use this early chapter to talk – just a little – about the brain.

AGE-OLD WISDOM AND THE LATEST NEUROSCIENCE

Modern brain research is gradually providing validation for ideas about human thinking that were intuited long ago. The thirteenth-century poet, Rumi, still immensely popular in various translations today, wrote much in his poems about different kinds of learning and attention. In one poem (called *Two Kinds of Intelligence* in Coleman Barks' lyrical version) he talks about two different kinds of knowing. One kind consists of facts and concepts, and with this intelligence we rise in the world. The other kind rests already within us, for us to tap into at any moment like drawing water from a flowing freshwater spring.

Now, 750 years later, neuroscience is constructing a narrative around the attention of the two hemispheres of the brain that looks remarkably similar to Rumi's description. The left hemisphere excels in pinning down meaning by building up a picture from facts and other evidence. The right hemisphere of the brain, on the other hand, maintains open, present awareness and has appreciation of a wider more comprehensive meaning, like a constant flowing fountain within.

Why Two Hemispheres?

If the human brain is all about connections with its millions of pathways, you might suppose that with time it might have gradually evolved into a single organ; but that hasn't happened. Not only are the two hemispheres of the brain slightly different shapes, left and right, up and down, front and back, but they are also separated from each other by the corpus callosum. This allows them to communicate with each other while also acting in some instances as an inhibitor to communication. The two hemispheres are irrevocably separate.

They are separate for a reason. As a general statement, the left hemisphere of your brain controls the right side of your body and the right hemisphere controls your left side. Over the past 50 years new information about the functioning of the brain has led us to realise that it's not quite as simple as that. We all use both sides of the brain (as indeed higher and lower, and posterior and anterior) for most activities, but there are quite clear demarcations for certain functions. Their *roles* are different.

Psychiatrist and writer Iain McGilchrist brings together recent discoveries in brain research in his ground-breaking book, *The Master and His Emissary*. He focuses on the *different qualities of attention* of the two hemispheres and shows how that attention radically changes our perception of the world.

Gilchrist acknowledges that we have critical need of both sides of the brain but suggests that we live increasingly and to our cost in a world that is hugely left-brained. The development of artificial intelligence can only increase this bias, and this presents dangers for communication and even for the future of the planet.

He is at pains to stress that his observations are generalisations, as individuals display many variations from the norm. However, for a huge percentage of the population they hold good. When, for whatever reason, only one side of the brain is available there are stark and consistent differences in how the subject interacts with the world.

The attention of the left-brain is immensely useful, and its skills are in use everywhere, from scientific enquiry to political theory to business strategy to leadership to verbal dexterity. However, it is only half-a-brain, and needs the balance of the right hemisphere to function well, as we see when we compare characteristics. Our choices about how we attend to the world, using the two hemispheres of our brain, affect what we actually find in that world; and what we find, in its turn, makes us into who we are – which then governs even more how we attend and what we notice and find … and so on.

LEFT HEMISPHERE

The left hemisphere employs logic and linear thinking with a narrow focus, grasping whatever details it deems to be relevant to its case, processing bits of information to build up a system of knowledge. It likes to pin things down, to deal with certainties and make things explicit, and sees the world in terms of absolutes: yes or no, right or wrong. It dislikes grey areas. It abstracts and generalises to create a representation or map, and manipulates data, even at times against experiential evidence, for internal coherence. It's useful for creating laws or business plans or financial models, and all areas of digital processing. However, its abstraction can on occasion lead to catastrophic results, as when algorithms that worked in the abstract utterly failed institutions in 2008 and facilitated the devastating financial crash.

Research on the individual hemispheres of split-brain patients (patients where the corpus callosum has been damaged or severed so that the two hemispheres cannot connect) shows that the left-brain on its own ignores evidence that it doesn't like or understand and invents things to make the evidence fit. Someone with access only to the left-brain is sure of her rightness and becomes angry if challenged. One patient who had lost control of her left side insisted that her own inert left arm resting on the bed belonged to someone in the bed with her and was quite insistent in her belief that if she had no control over the arm, it didn't belong to her.

The left-brain has a major input in speech and language but takes the world literally; it is expert on internal logic and syntax but not on meaning. When the left-brain of a split-brain patient was isolated, she could name a pencil but couldn't say what it was for. Using just the right hemisphere she knew what it was for but not its name. The left-brain can happily use abstract words such as progress or equality and assume a consistent meaning, whereas the right brain realises that such words hold a multiplicity of shades of meaning. If someone tells a joke, it takes the lateral thinking of the right-brain to catch the humour; the left-brain needs the joke to be explained.

Certainty and simple explanations make the left-brain powerful. It follows a line of reasoning, building confidence in the argument as it goes. The micro-control and lack of trust we find in the industrial world today are left-brain attributes that lead towards rigidity and despotism. The left-brain doesn't realise its own limitations: it thinks it is the master of the universe.

RIGHT HEMISPHERE

Unlike the left hemisphere with its manipulation of pieces of data, the right hemisphere absorbs information as a whole by maintaining present awareness with a broad focus, without any preconception of what may or may not be found.

With a greater understanding of the whole, it comes at the truth by means of intuition, imagination, and, crucially, a feel for context. It has a greater sense of complexity, nuance, implicit meaning, and the uniqueness of each experience. Where the left-brain would be more likely to categorise: for example, I am the expert, you are the client, the right-brain finds connection: I am a (unique and individual) human and you are a (unique and individual) human. It shows more spontaneity and willingness to trust than the left hemisphere. Metaphor, symbol, paradox and humour are all its province. Being in this more complex space, although the right-brain has a more holistic comprehension of reality, it doesn't assume it knows everything, and so is more open to doubt. That is its problem; it has neither the certainty nor the language to make itself heard in a left-brain world.

A very simple way to describe the differences would be to see the left-brain as experience (it learns from the known) and the right brain as experienc-*ing* (it *lives* actual experience). In another analogy, the left-brain is sense (as in making sense of) and the right brain is sens-*ing* (as in being aware of).

IDEAL RELATIONSHIP BETWEEN HEMISPHERES

We need a balance between the two hemispheres for us to thrive. It is quite clear, however, that in the Western world the left-brain is constantly given precedence. The Nobel Prize-winning neuropsychologist Roger Sperry, who did important research on split-brain patients, worried that both science and our education system neglect and discriminate against the right-brain's nonverbal form of intellect. McGilchrist goes further, to assert that both hemispheres of the brain are essential but that the right-brain has a better holistic understanding of the role of both and needs, therefore, to be the prime hemisphere. Albert Einstein held a similar view. 'The intuitive mind is a sacred gift and the rational mind is a faithful servant', he stated, making clear which he thought should be pre-eminent.

After reading my summary of the characteristics of the two hemispheres of the brain, you may have already reflected that, while we all have need of left-brain characteristics and use them all the time, right-brain characteristics are particularly important for certain kinds of communication.

Have a look at the differences between the two hemispheres' ways of attending in table form on the following pages.

You can see that the left-brain, like Rumi's first kind of learning, attends to learning as the accumulation of knowledge. The right-brain thinks of it more as clearing away impediments to understanding. The director Sam Mendes once praised the actor Judi Dench for her ability to *reveal herself* in acting rather than adding masks, as others were wont to do. Getting real in communication is about peeling off layers, not about adding more. It's *un-learning,* not acquiring. The biggest difference between the old method and the new in communication is in how you learn. In the old method you added new skills; in the new, you take away – you *remove* blocks and inhibitions.

As we tend to be driven by habit, this unlearning can feel strange and counter-intuitive, and certainly not what we might understand as learning. It's about thinking less rather than more. It's about following your inner voice as much as your habitual rational sense.

LEFT HEMISPHERE		RIGHT HEMISPHERE	
Right side of body – 'stronger'		Left side of body – 'weaker'	
ATTENTION			
Focus – specifics. Builds from facts/evidence;		**Open, present awareness.** Alert, holistic;	
knows what it's looking for		no idea what it's looking for	
MEANING, PURPOSE			
Grasps, makes a case, pins down certainty.		**Meaning implicit, complex.** Possibilities nuanced.	
Exclusive – yes/no, either/or; literal.		Inclusive – both/and; contextual.	
Manipulation, persuasion; control/power		**Connection; understanding;** human values	
METHOD			
Abstracts and generalises – map of territory; wrests from context, categorises;		**Attends to present actuality** – unique terrain	
Sees what it expects, relies on what it knows		No expectation, everything new	
Targets, algorithms, systems, procedures, tasks, behaviours;		Subtlety, feel of context, symbol, metaphor, humour paradox, lateral thinking;	
Linear logical path irrespective of context, even against experience; planned, organised, ideal;		Learning complex and contextual; spontaneous, intuition; flow, what matters, messy reality;	
Questions to find bits of info – clarity, proof		Questions to discover meaning, value	
Doing		Being	

LEFT HEMISPHERE	RIGHT HEMISPHERE
RELATIONSHIP	
Detachment prime, no felt sense of relationship; dissociated	**Relationship** prime, meaning from connection; in between-ness
Social emotion, especially anger/judgement; generic	**Complex emotions**, empathy; personal; self-aware, reads faces (eyes)
Most interested in machines, made-made; not so concerned with others or feelings	Most interested in living things; well disposed towards others
Linguistic – words count	**Meaning often nonverbal**
CONFIDENCE	
Zero doubt, but self-deceiving; invents when can't understand or for consistency; angry if challenged; isolation and rigidity when struggling	**Tentative at times, but more true.** Aware of complexity so never 100% sure; greater acceptance of difference; fear and overwhelm when struggling
Despotic, self-sufficient	**Realises need both hemispheres**
Doesn't realise own limitations	Greater understanding and the better leader

Whole Mind Thinking

The wisdom to communicate successfully with each other requires both hemispheres of our brain. We are quite used to this idea of both in the case of our eyes. Each eye sees a slightly but distinctly different image, yet we are able to use this important difference to see in three dimensions and get a perspective on what we see. This is no small advantage and it comes about *because* of differences.

The left hemisphere on its own often shows little wisdom. It tends to tackle problems with energy and a desire for effectiveness but without sufficient systemic or lateral thinking – and often sacrifices human kindness for efficiency.

How many times have you heard someone of great seniority declare that *lessons will be learned* after something has gone seriously wrong? Then corrective procedures are put in place that lead in a straight line from problem to solution, ignoring by-products that could sabotage success further down the line.

Shutting the Stable Door After the Horse has Bolted

 When the Irish troubles were at their height and the IRA was threatening London, an IRA bomb, thought to have been secreted into the Tower of London in a tourist's bag, caused many injuries and one death. About this time, I used to take visitors to the Tower on a regular basis, and for months and years after the bomb blast tourists used to have to queue while officials implemented their new safety measure – to search every bag. Only bags though. You could have arrived wearing a huge coat with ample pockets like Fagin in *Oliver Twist* and officials would still check only your bag, as that was the solution devised to fix the particular problem.

The Law of Unintended Consequences

 Several years ago, the UK Government brought in a new inducement for schools in order to favour parental choice. Those schools that achieved good results were to be given extra funding, while those that did less well would be denied funding – a perfect left-brain solution to under-achievement. As suspected by many, the thriving schools continued to improve and increase in student numbers, thus attracting further funding, while the schools denied funding declined even further and often ended up in special measures. 'You could see it coming, not a great help for parental choice', commented a teacher friend wryly.

Not put off by the negative results of such a scheme, a more recent government offered extra funding to *hospitals* that succeed in balancing their books. The hospitals in more needy areas that fail to balance the books are denied this extra funding, which of course makes it even harder for them to balance the books the next year, creating a continuous declining spiral. *Plus ça change!*

It's not enough to correct a procedure and produce a new rule. Wisdom uses creativity and wider, deeper perception to examine a problem holistically and embraces a plethora of possibilities to find the way forward. Sometimes, instead of the complete restructure so favoured by left-brain thinking, a right-brain solution, after examining all possibilities, may be a small tweak that affects all parts of the existing system.

A Systemic Tweak

An example of a 'tweak' was the simple reintroduction of one species, the wolf, into Yellowstone, which had a huge impact on the biodiversity of the Park. The over-large elk population began to avoid grazing in regions where they could be easily challenged by wolves, and as a result various plants were given the opportunity to flourish in those places. The new vegetation had an impact on the rivers, and that affected other species, increasing the variety of birds and numbers of rabbits and mice. Beavers returned to the park and their dams attracted otters, muskrats, and reptiles. The whole eco-system found a richer balance.

Much that is endangering the planet is caused by left-brain thinking that tends to isolate actions in boxes and concentrate with narrow focus on the problem in hand. With this approach, it finds it easy to plunder the planet for resources, or fight for land, oil or water, or exploit people for increased total gain, or emphasise individual autonomy and success at the expense of the whole. We need to remember our holistic right-brain vision that takes in the whole in a caring glance. Our right-brain doesn't work things out step by step; it allows the other-than-conscious mind to scan the whole picture and then flies to an intuition based on the whole.

So, let us look at the alternative world of real communication and see how our right-brain adds something new and vital to our interactions with each other.

2

BE AN AWAKENER

> *There are many whose eyes are awake*
> *while their heart is asleep.*
> *And what do they see?*
> *But those who keep their heart awake,*
> *will open the eyes of a hundred more.*
> – Rumi

You wake up body and mind. As you let go, your breath releases a well of energy. Your body relaxes and becomes free to move with economy and grace, at one with thought and intention. This in turn frees your voice to vibrate in harmony with other people. You are joyfully alive to others and show up authentically.

Awaken Your Life Energy

Energy might not seem an obvious place to start. After all, how much energy does is take to talk to someone? But one of the features you may notice about controlled communication is the lack of life. And one of the reasons people love spontaneity is because it is alive and real. Spontaneous people seem more intensely awake and happier in their own skin than other people, and you feel drawn to their strong life force. The art of meaningful communication starts from this powerful source of relational energy, for it transmits to others and encourages them too to be awake, present, and alive.

'Unbeingdead isn't beingalive', quips the poet e e cummings. It's not just physical energy. With certain people you feel an infectious spark starting with their eyes, which lights up the room. You get a sense of someone who is fully present and alive, acting with flexibility and lightness. You suspect they might say or do something interesting or new and you want to be there when it happens.

For many people, life consists of living unchanging daily routines with the same people, having similar thoughts and feelings day after day. Others are in a worried or conflicted state which saps their energy and makes them think that they need more rest – which drains their energy even more. When energy is blocked, true feeling, good thinking and spontaneous action are blocked too. But for those who are truly alive, awake in body, heart and mind, every conversation is the flow of a new adventure, with fresh unknowns offering new possibility, powered by a vibrant energy that springs from within – their life force.

Famous Performers

 Some people's life force is palpable. People who saw Marlon Brando in Tennessee Williams' *A Streetcar Named Desire* felt a huge energy emanating from him. When the cellist Pablo Casals played his music, a quality from somewhere deep within him touched and energised the listener with something more powerful than mere pleasure and admiration. Stevie Wonder attracts the highest praise from the greatest musicians of our time as a force of nature who inspired them in their own careers. Mariah Carey called him, 'the most incredible singer songwriter in history and one of the most beautiful spirits in the entire world'.

As we've seen, many comedians radiate huge energy with fast-paced routines, brisk patter, and energetic movement. But it's one thing to tell a previously learned joke with flair; it's another to be able to respond hilariously in the wink of an eye to something unexpected. Some comedians emanate energy that turns everything they touch into comic gold. Looking back along the years, I think of Victoria Wood with her lightening quick mind, Lee Mack revelling in his instant humour to suit any situation, or Spike Milligan's huge enjoyment of his own mad humour spilling over into spontaneous giggles. You'll have your own examples.

Life energy creates on the spot, improvises, and extemporises. When you have a conversation with someone who possesses such an inner spark, talk flows, and pleases, and surprises.

Attempts have been made throughout the ages to describe man's life force or inner energy. One of the earliest is the *Hymn of Creation* from the *Rig Veda* written 3000 years ago, which states that, 'In the beginning there was neither existence nor non-existence; all this world was unmanifest energy'.

'Energy is all there is', claimed Albert Einstein. 'Energy is delight', wrote poet and mystic William Blake. e. e. Cummings' joyful life force leaps out of the page in his poem 'i thank You God for most this amazing'. 'I believe a leaf of grass is no less than the journey-work of the stars,' writes Walt Whitman in his long poem, 'Song of Myself', where every line expresses his huge expansive energy.

Gerald Manley Hopkins captures the heartfelt energy in his description of a kestrel in flight:

> High there, how he rung upon the rein of a wimpling wing
> In his ecstasy! then off, off forth on swing,
> As a skate's heel sweeps smooth on a bow-bend: the hurl and gliding
> Rebuffed the big wind. My heart in hiding
> Stirred for a bird, — the achieve of; the mastery of the thing!

The choreographer Martha Graham suggests:

> There is a vitality, a life force, an energy, a quickening that is translated through you into action, and because there is only one of you in all time, this expression is unique.

Watch a young child at play, and there it is in action – exhilarating fresh energy and focus on the activity of the moment. Boundless joyful energy is our natural state, mind, body and spirit all involved.

ACCESS THROUGH THE BODY

We all have potential access to this inner energy, but it's often trapped and blocked. When you communicate with people you can sense blocked energy in their lack of spontaneity and interest.

Alive and Un-Dead

 Recently, I accompanied my daughter to hospital for a minor operation. The reception area was not busy, but the receptionist was offhand. She said what she needed to say and did what she was

---

meant to do, but we remarked afterwards that she hadn't even seen us, let alone connected with us. Her energy was dense and lifeless, and focused on her task, not on relationship.

Later, in the tense time just before the operation, a nurse came into the room and connected with empathy straightaway, understanding the situation and offering encouraging words. Everything about her spoke life. The receptionist as a person was absent, leaving just the automatic responses of her role; the nurse was real and present. Both members of staff had done their job, but the difference was huge.

Access Your Life Energy

 When you pay attention quietly, you can feel your life energy.

- Stand or sit with your arms loose at your sides or separated on your lap. Close your eyes or soften your gaze.
- Move your attention to your hands and become aware of the life in them – you may feel a slight tingling sensation. Stay focused on them and notice the feeling grow.
- Allow this tingling/alive feeling to expand slowly up your arms into your chest, through your body, down to your toes and right up into your head. Feel your

whole body glowing with tingling life energy like a huge smile across your chest.

- Extend the sensation beyond the boundaries of your body into the space around you. You may like to move your arms and whole body gently in space to amplify the sensation.

Take notice of the times when you feel most energised. When you dance or go for a run, you can feel tired afterwards but pleased and energised at the same time with endorphins coursing through you. You can feel enlivened when you listen to music. You may feel a rush of energy as you enthusiastically contemplate a new idea that's suddenly come to you. You feel a similar glow of excitement and surge of vitality when you have a deeply satisfying conversation with a friend. Catch that feeling when it occurs and notice its effect on your physiology and state of mind.

DIFFERENT FROM MANIC OR EGOTISTICAL ENERGY

Life force is not the same as plain high energy. Some public figures and presenters assault you with high decibels and provocative energy. You're certainly aware of their power, but it's egotistical and jarring, their bodies top-heavy with effort and their voices loud and untuneful. Some energy is violent and destructive. Think of certain assertive wartime leaders whipping up crowd energy at mass rallies or certain presenters of television programmes who exploit energy without subtlety. You may know someone who engages you in conversation like this. They enter your space without permission and you feel assaulted.

There's a huge difference between exhausting egotistical energy and resonant energy that's glowing and contagious. Some people give out energy; others suck it in. An energetic person does not always energise. In fact, all too often, someone with huge energy and lots of talk who is at the centre of every group seizes all the attention and enervates everyone else. When a certain well-known comedian appears on a panel show, he grabs the initiative and his fellow comedians on the show lose their natural humour as he exhausts them in his unwillingness to work cooperatively. In contrast, a young person I know creates joy and lightness wherever she goes and people are attracted by her energy. Think of different people you know, and you can see which way it goes. One sucks all the energy into itself, 'consuming your essence', as Rumi put it, the other uses energy to resonate with others and lift their energy too.

Immediate energetic reactions can also be the result of compulsion – like an addict grabbing a drink, triggered by the primitive part of the brain. A response clicks in automatically, triggered by habit, bypassing thinking or caring. Another energetic response is produced by impulsiveness, stemming from a rash, 'what the hell' desperation associated with low self-esteem, causing the person to do something reckless or violent. Some people, having seen what can be gained by it, adopt a persona that exhibits fake energy or buffoonery.

Any of these examples of forced or manic high energy may stir you with their desire to shock and draw attention to themselves, but more often they enervate. Life force, on the other hand, is relational; it invigorates and inspires. Those who bring their life force to conversation create lightness and even joy. You get the sense of a lively brain, a ready heart and a pulsating soul, which create a direct line to the subconscious much quicker and surer than conscious thinking. You need this inner energy to engage and connect with people at deeper levels. 'Anything or anyone that does not bring you alive is too small for you', says the poet David Whyte.

ALERT *AND* RELAXED

Your life force cannot be forced or controlled; it can only be discovered within yourself, like a vibrating wheel of energy. It is a union of opposites: you come closest to it when you are both acutely alert and beautifully relaxed at the same time.

COUNTER–INTUITION

Access high energy AND deep relaxation at the same time.

Alert doesn't mean stressed and relaxed doesn't mean slumped. You feel a mental alertness opening through your body, reflected in an expansion of your mind; at the same time you feel at ease, relaxed. In this state you are able to let others in.

Successful sportsmen recognise exactly this combination of high energy and deep relaxation when they perform 'in the zone'. Try the following two practice exercises to experience both at the same time; you may find one practice works better for you than the other.

High Energy and Deep Relaxation

- **High energy**

    Remember a time when you were highly energised and enjoying yourself. Feel again the sensation of power and the thrill of that time. When that feeling is at its strongest, raise your dominant hand to touch your upper chest. Enjoy the sensation of energy.

- Lower your hand and return to the present moment.
- **Beautiful relaxation**

    Now remember a time when you were beautifully relaxed, enjoying the peace of the moment. Feel again that exquisite sense of calm. When the feeling is at its most relaxed and peaceful, raise your non-dominant hand to touch your upper chest. Enjoy that beautiful calm.

- Lower your hand and return to the present moment.
- **Both energised and relaxed**

    Now raise both hands to your upper chest, one on top of the other over your heart, and feel both sensations at the same time. Experience the power of their fusion.

It helps if you have a friend to read the instructions to you, so that you can focus completely on the sensations. The exercise works particularly well if you perform it with the help of two other people, one to remind you of high energy and touch your right shoulder for a few moments; and then the other to remind you of beautiful relaxation and touch your left shoulder for a few moments. Finally, they both touch the shoulder they touched before, but at the same time as each other, to meld two different states of mind.

Aikido Practice: Unbendable Arm

This exercise from the peaceful martial art of Aikido is suitable for beginners and a perfect demonstration of the power of energy and relaxation combined.

If someone tries to bend your arm when it is stiff, they succeed if they're as strong as you. But when your arm is relaxed, they can't do it!

You need a partner. Here's the process:

- **Tight arm:** Hold one arm straight out horizontally with a tight fist. Your partner places one hand on top of the underside of your elbow and the other under your wrist and then gradually tries to bend your arm. They will usually succeed if they are as strong as you.
- **Relaxed arm:** Hold the arm out again with all your muscles relaxed and your wrist dangling a little, using just enough strength to keep your arm in the air.
- Look out in the direction of your arm and imagine the powerful energy of a beam of light extending out from your fingers into the far distance. (Imagine

a powerful hose of water if you prefer.) Stay powerfully with this feeling while your partner attempts to bend your arm again. Impossible!

Magic, isn't it? Energy and relaxation at the same time. You are *more* powerful when you are relaxed.

NB: Don't use excessive force when you perform this exercise on someone's rigid arm; you will feel distinctly the difference between a tight arm and a relaxed arm without either of you having to exert undue force.

Breathe for Energy and Flow

Your life force is intimately connected with your breath. Every sound you make, every action you take, depends on an intake of air for its energy. When you breathe in deeply, you expand your consciousness and think more clearly. Changing your breathing changes what's possible for you.

BREATHING IN ANCIENT SYSTEMS

From the 2000-year-old Vedic tradition of the world starting with the god Brahma's giant out-breath, breathing has been the vital element of life force energy. The Japanese talk of Ki, the Chinese of Qi, the Hawaiians of Mana. Indians refer to prana.

We can choose to tap into this flow of energy or not. When our Ki is strong, we feel confident and ready to enjoy life and take on challenges. When it is low, we feel weak and are more likely to get sick. We receive Ki from food, sunshine, sleep, and especially from the air we breathe. It's possible to increase our Ki by using breathing exercises and meditation.

E. Herrigel describes in *Zen in the Art of Archery* how an apprentice in the art of archery used to learn breathing exercises before anything else.

In Aikido, you access Ki or universal energy through the combination of relaxation and alertness as I've described. Relaxation allows the energy to flow through your body with the breath to where it is needed at any time. Your quality of attention allows you to access the energy as required. The energy is then focused on your intention.

Students of T'ai Chi do something similar. They learn how to access the state of careful attention together with intention. Calm movement with slow breathing on the outside relaxes and calms the spirit and re-energises and focuses the mind. This energy with focus on the inside produces graceful effective movement and creative thought – life force in action. Many claim that the Ki of martial arts masters is so strong that it affects the world around them, so that an attacker feels the master's force and falls before he is even physically touched.

Many traditions suggest that a main cause of disease – dis-ease – is a disruption in the flow of Ki or breath energy through the body. Ki is blocked by negative thoughts and feelings. We know through a whole body of research that our physical and mental performance is strongly affected by our thoughts and feelings. The neuroscientist Candace Pert asserted that the mysterious life force's subtle energy is actually the free flow of information, carried without blocks or interference, by the biochemicals of emotion, the neuropeptides and their receptors.

We say that we breathe but that's not quite true: rather, life breathes us. Observe someone's breath and you learn much about their inner world; every emotion or physical trauma alters a person's breathing. Anxiety inhibits the breath; relief frees the breath immediately. Virginia Woolf described this sensation of relief when she received good news after a friend's operation in hospital: 'Curious how all one's fibres seem to expand and fill with air when anxiety is taken off.'

When your breath blocks, your mind and body block and energy is blocked. Many of us acquired a habit of breathing shallowly as children. If we were instructed not to cry or want or protest or run or dance for joy, the restrictions resulted in repressed breathing which, if not addressed, then carried on into adulthood. When you communicate, breath is key. As soon as you feel stressed, you breathe shallowly, and therefore lack energy and a clear mind. Take a good breath and your mind clears again.

Breath is part of both the automatic response system and the voluntary response system, so we can influence our breath intentionally for greater health and energy and to change our state. Many voice and singing experts have written on how to take a large breath. When we empty our lungs fully while staying open and relaxed, the in-breath happens on its own as a *release*, with zero effort and a wonderful sense of liberation. The lungs get to do what they naturally want to do, which is to fill with air after they have emptied. Similarly, after we sigh, the whole respiratory system is able to release and reset with the in-breath.

So, breathe! Especially breathe out fully to allow an ample in-breath. When you are tense, breathe! When you feel awkward, breathe! When a conversation falters, breathe! And things become easier again.

Breathing practices help, so here are a few to choose from.

Breathe like a Cat in Repose

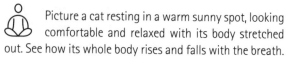 Picture a cat resting in a warm sunny spot, looking comfortable and relaxed with its body stretched out. See how its whole body rises and falls with the breath.

For this exercise, lie stretched out in a comfortable warm place. Feel open and relaxed. Imagine you are that cat in the sunshine, enjoying the beautiful relaxation of your whole body and the gentle rise and fall of your breath – nothing to do, nowhere to go, just the pleasure of this luxurious moment and the feeling of effortless flowing movement. The breath comes into your body like a caress. It might even make you smile. It's amazing how *little* you need to do to breathe fully.

Ha Energy Breathing

My yoga teacher, Louise Ionascu, employs this practice to celebrate fuller conscious breathing and build joyful energy. For this practice, stand easily with soft knees and swing rhythmically and freely from position to position. Your feet stay in one place about hips-width apart throughout the movement.

- Swing your arms forward to chest height, palms down, as you take a rapid sip of air through the nose with a sniff.

- Swing arms out to the side with a rhythmical small dip of the knees as you sniff in a bit of extra air without breathing out first.
- With another little dip, swing your arms rhythmically up over your head, palms facing forwards, as you take a final sip of air to top up.
- Then let everything release, swinging your arms forwards and down to sweep back past your knees, as your body goes into a forward bend with bent knees. At the same time you expel the air all at once through your mouth with a vigorous 'haaaaa!'
- Move straight into swinging the arms forward again and repeat the exercise several times rhythmically. Find a pace that suits you. It might vary on different days.
- At the end, remain in the forward bend for a few moments and observe. Allow your breath to normalise.
- Finally, come slowly back to standing and notice how invigorated you feel.

If you are not used to full breathing you might get a bit light headed, in which case rest for a few moments before resuming.

Breathing Out to a Count

The talented conductor and teacher Amy Bebbington shared this simple practice that encourages the *relaxed* drawing-in of energy with the in-breath.

It relies on slow steady counting throughout. Try to empty yourself of air on each out-breath.

- Allow air to fill your lungs and release the tummy to a count of 1. Your mouth and tongue should be naturally free of tension.
- Hiss steadily to the sound *Ss* for the count of 4. The belly button will naturally move towards your spine as the air is expelled. Remember not to tighten in the body, face, or jaw when expelling your air.
- Repeat the first step to fill with air to the count of 1.
- Hiss for the count of 6.
- Repeat the sequence, gradually increasing the exhalation counts in multiples of 2, according to your natural capacity.

Stay within your own limits, so that you don't strain. Relax your shoulders! Remember the in-breath is a letting go. Your ability will improve with gentle repetition.

ENERGY EXPRESSES ITSELF IN JOY, AND JOY ENERGISES

When you are overflowing with vitality, not only do you feel great and flourish, but you also feel lighter and less inclined to take yourself too seriously.

Instead of fighting what is, know that you're on the river of life flowing downstream, and each moment will be experienced and then passed by. The wisest character in a Shakespeare play is not the hero but the Fool. As you lighten up, you lighten up those around you, and your whole environment becomes more awake and open to possibility. When you bring this spirit to your inter-actions with other people, it gives you the mental flexibility to twist and weave, to think with a lively fresh mind and arrive at somewhere new.

The Piano Staircase

 It's extraordinary how fun changes people's mindset. In an experiment, people from *The Fun Theory* painted a stairway up from the under-ground railway so that each step looked like a note on a giant piano. Then they set it up so that each step played a note of the scale as people trod on it.

Tired-looking commuters had the choice of using the escalator or climbing the 'piano staircase' next to it. In a break from their usual routine, the majority spontaneously elected to climb the stairs rather than use the escalator because it looked like fun. Many even experimented with different ways to 'play' the steps or 'danced' their way up. You can enjoy it on YouTube at: http://www.youtube.com/watch?v=2lXh2n0aPyw.

We often feel that our energy is finite and gets used up, but a major part of energy is our state of mind.

There's a wonderful word, 'galumphing', usually applied to children or baby animals, that describes a purposeless superfluity of activity – such as hopping or skipping instead of walking; balancing along a wall instead of keeping to the ground; or creating deliberate obstacles to make one's passage interesting. Children learn later to follow set rules, but in galumphing they are exploring and playing. They learn, not only to ride a bike, but to be able to shout, 'Look, no hands!' Thus, too, in the best conversations, we search, experiment, and tread lightly – there are few rules there either.

I can hear someone protest that nothing at work is about having fun. But look around you and you will notice people who tread lightly even in the workplace, and often achieve more than those who carry a visible weight of seriousness on their shoulders.

There's no right and wrong in having fun; there's no such thing as a mistake. No one tries hard at it either. This is a huge concern in conversation, where inhibition or ideas of 'rightness' can easily stunt the flow. We literally forget how to laugh and play. It's interesting isn't it, that a musical instrument is always 'played'? It's never 'worked'.

WHAT BRINGS YOU ALIVE?

Everything you love to do energises you. One part of re-energising yourself, as we've seen, is enjoying your physicality – moving your body in dance and other activities, enjoying walking in nature, building skill in a sport.

Achievement of the just-achievable is another powerful energiser: when you undertake a challenge only just within your capability and feel wonderful afterwards; when you win in a sport against a worthwhile opponent; or when you make a phone call you find daunting and feel as strong as a lion afterwards.

Another part is cultivating awe – that feeling that permeates your being when you hear a beautiful piece of music, read a moving poem, look at an uplifting picture or grand building, or read a book that inspires you. Noticing little miracles achieves it too. If the sun suddenly bursts out from behind a cloud, you take a second to appreciate it. If you suddenly spot a deer in nature, you register your delight. If a view suddenly takes your breath away, you notice that bigger breath of pleasure that follows.

Whenever you do something that has strong meaning for you, or come up with a fresh idea, you feel energy coursing through you. Such energy is a powerful attractor for others.

Joyful activity – even activity that uses loads of energy – *energises*, and you feel livelier afterwards rather than tired. 'He who kisses the joy as it flies lives in eternity's sun rise', wrote William Blake. The fourteenth-century Sufi poet Hafez found his ecstasy in dancing and wrote in a poem: 'If you think I am having more fun than anyone on this planet you are absolutely correct.'

Nothing energises us more than finding enjoyment in something for its own sake. Watch the grace and ease with which Nicola Benedetti plays the violin, her face reflecting her total absorption and enjoyment. She certainly isn't disturbing her focus by thinking about how others perceive her. The Brazilian football star, Pelé, described the experience of being vitally alive on match days, feeling that he could run all day without getting tired and pass every member of the opposition without difficulty.

Finally, one of the best energisers is the buzz you get from an open and true conversation with someone.

Here are a couple of simple practices to help you capture this joyful energy.

Awaken Your Joyful Life Force

- Remember a time in your life when – through joy, or delighted surprise, or excitement – you had energy in such abundance that it seemed to overflow. You felt like running and jumping; you wanted to laugh with high spirits; you were in love with life. At such a time you were in touch with your life force. For many people, it's a while since they felt that way – maybe not even since childhood. That's fine: remember a time in your childhood.

- Settle into yourself for a moment and relive the time you were bubbling with energy. Visualise everything you were seeing at the time. Are the colours bright or pastel, light or dark? Listen to the sounds of the time, in the foreground and background. Are they loud or soft, or is there silence? What feeling suffuses your body? Enjoy it fully.

- Take a joyful breath filling yourself with the memory and feel how it opens your whole body. Sense how it produces a feeling of confidence and energy in the here and now. Capture all elements of the feeling and know that you can return to it when you want.

Let Go

We access high energy only when our minds and bodies are free and relaxed. Having energy is very different from expending effort. Deep in many of us there lurks a private conviction that nothing worthwhile is achieved without hard work. The conviction leads us to extraordinary contradictions. We *work hard* for peace; we *beat ourselves up* to relax more; we *worry* about our serenity of mind; and we *thrash ourselves* in the gym to acquire ease in our bodies. None of these efforts is energising when approached as hard work.

The more we wrestle with ideas in our minds and the more we exert effort, the more physical tension we have in our bodies. I was interested to discover that most people move more rigidly on their dominant, 'try hard' side. When we frown, clench our teeth, or tighten our jaw we create resistance against ourselves that makes everything harder. It's like pushing and pulling at the same time. We find ourselves unable to think clearly or make headway in whatever we are doing. Paradoxically, this triggers more effort to think, which causes the rational part of our brain to make ever greater conscious effort.

Communicating with others is certainly less productive if you try too hard. The only solution is to let go. But how can you do that when communication and relationships with others matter and you want things to go well? To most of us, the idea of letting go is associated with giving up and we fear that it would be a disaster. We have lots of baggage around keeping going, maintaining standards, fighting the good fight, continuing the struggle, and refusing to surrender. It takes a special type of courage to let go of your usual anchors and props.

COUNTER-INTUITION

The act of stepping off the edge gives you wings.

LET GO PHYSICALLY

We sometimes talk about tension as if it's nothing to do with us – a tense meeting, a tense atmosphere – but tension is in people. Someone who is uptight is exactly that – shoulders up and body tight. We express ourselves from moment to moment in our voice, movement, breathing, and in micro-movements such as signing our name. When we're out of flow, we drop things and trip up; our signature becomes cramped or shaky.

So, letting go physically is the first challenge. Whether your feelings inside are pleasurable or uncomfortable, pay attention to releasing any associated physical tension. With each new breath, release every part of your body more and more. As you let go physically, the feelings that cause tension – principally fear – are also released, and gradually you dissolve the armour you have built up to protect you from other people. There's a softening inside you, the physical release leading the way to an awakening of your spirit.

As you soften, you begin to feel again, and become more yourself. Whatever was numb in you comes back to life. As the tightness dissolves, so does the rigidity of any roles you are attempting to maintain, which take much of your energy. Many Eastern disciplines teach that body awareness and relaxation is the route to better thinking; deep concentration is possible when you are present and aware in your body.

As you let go and relax, you become ever more sensitive to what is happening in your body as you listen to it without trying to control it. You may feel the pulsing of anxiety or shakiness, even tearfulness, but stay with it. It opens our understanding to what we feel and releases us from having to restrict our feelings to those we think are appropriate.

Of course, feeling again is scary, which is why so many people try to exert control. To let go is to be willing to feel your pain. Unwillingness to feel pain is what causes you to resist. But listening to your body and feeling again is vital for your health and wellbeing and for your emotional connection with other people. You don't need to examine or talk *about* feelings: it is enough to *feel*.

Letting go physically enables you to let go mentally of various gremlins: all those musts, shoulds, dos, and don'ts and the need to be right or rigidly consistent. So, you let go, not knowing whether you'll fall or fly and, free of blocks, inhibitions, and agendas, your inner energy is released and you soar.

Sky-Gazing

The British artist J. M. W. Turner recorded that he used to spend hours in his childhood simply lying on his back staring into the sky. His indolence served him well. During his lifetime, he produced 550 oil paintings, 2000 watercolours and 30 000 paper works, many of them exceptional pieces of art. Profitable sky-gazing, you might say, worth letting go.

Relax in Company

For the best of motives, it's common to make an extra effort when we meet people, and this causes us to stiffen up. This practice is to meet someone or walk into a room of people and stay *physically relaxed*.

- Have no expectation either of yourself or anyone else. Don't run away from any discomfort. Whatever you feel, whether fear or awkwardness, just breathe and relax with every out-breath.
- Congratulate yourself for every moment that you experience a feeling of being relaxed.
- Become curious about what happens, and what is different when you let go – even a little.
- Afterwards, reflect on how the encounter went when you were more relaxed.

Realise that the conscious mind can't do conversation well on its own. We have to find ways to hand over to the other-than-conscious mind and trust it to give us the grace to know what to say and how to say it. Letting go and going with the flow allow creative insights to well up in the mind.

FREE THE VOICE

There are few aspects of communication more important that your voice. I'm sure there have been times when you've been put off by the sound of someone's voice: by someone mumbling as if they couldn't be bothered to make the effort to reach you, or by a harshness of tone that assaulted your ears like a physical attack. Maybe you've found yourself not trusting someone because their voice sounded tense or artificial? Your right-brain understands sound and is not deceived by mere words. I've written extensively elsewhere about voice, so I'll describe some aspects just briefly here.

When you speak to someone, the process starts with your intention, that tiny seed of energy/feeling/desire/idea to communicate something. The intention prompts you to take a breath. That breath contains in it the energy of your feeling/desire/idea. If that energy is delight, you naturally take a full and free breath that gives your words a warm vibrant sound. If the feeling/desire/idea is strong disagreement, you breathe in firmly and rapidly, which produces a firm resolute sound in response.

Intention → breath → sound

Voice is vibration, and you connect through sharing that vibration in sound. That's where the real meaning of your utterance lies: underneath the words you use. Every intention produces a variation in the kind of energy you invest in taking breath, and this in turn makes your voice resonate in different parts of your body and sound different for each expression. So, although it's perfectly possible to breathe badly, there isn't one correct way to take a breath. For each thought and feeling our frame adjusts itself in a different way to take a breath. These different breaths enliven your communication and lend it variety and subtlety. Or at least, this is what happens *if we don't interfere with the process.*

All too often, we do: we interrupt the natural progression from in-breath to expression – the true response – and pause for a micro-second after taking in air for our conscious mind to exert control over what we say. This is the left-brain in action. Instead of our words coming out spontaneously, they are inhibited by inner imperatives such as to be careful, sound authoritative, hide our anger, and so on. That tiny hiatus before speech breaks the flow from the original energy to its expression, and the resulting sound fails to express our inner emotional energy. It then sounds flat and dull, tight, measured, or consciously manipulated to express something. When that happens, we fail to sound interesting to others. If such hiatus becomes a habit, our body adjusts into a settled, stiff arrangement of throat, chest and abdomen and the monotony of our voice reflects this rigidity.

The fact that this happens exposes the absurdity of creating procedures for spoken human interactions, such as the unadorned instruction to service staff to wish each customer 'Have a nice day' or 'Enjoy your meal'. It also exposes the false jollity of TV commercials, let alone the cheeriness of the recorded voice on a railway platform. Without meaning invested in the sound, words are empty shells, and people hear this in the quality of tone. How long does it take you to recognise a telephone advertising call when you pick up the phone – one second maybe?

Voice of Inner Resolve

 Intention is all. I sometimes used to talk crossly and stridently to my children. I'd snap, 'Don't do that!' or 'Come away from there!' to ever-diminishing effect. Then sometimes a resolve took hold inside me, and I would think to myself with a kind of internal knowing, 'This is enough. I truly am not going to allow this anymore.' What came out of my mouth then was something quieter, firmer, and slower, from deep in my body. And when that happened, the children took my words very seriously indeed. I was frequently surprised by their reaction because I hadn't been thinking about putting on a particular voice; I had merely changed my intention.

The Mature Child

 I witnessed the clear connection between intention and voice recently in the simplest of settings, when a TV reporter interviewed a child living on an isolated farm in the Outer Hebrides. The child responded to questions articulately and intelligently without self-consciousness, like someone well beyond his years. It was shocking really how *unusual* this felt – the transparency and power of it without the usual self-consciousness, timidity, subterfuge, or sophistication that most of us learn through early life experience, education and the media.

When your voice connects directly to breath and intention, its meaning reaches the listener directly and cleanly with no gap between person and language. The voice coach Kristin Linklater in her book *Freeing the Natural Voice* calls this a *transparent* voice, that 'reveals, not describes, inner impulses of emotion and thought, directly and spontaneously'. Maybe this is the reason that people have always responded positively and enthusiastically to singers such as Edith Piaf – whose voice no one would call beautiful, but whose sound touched the inner core of her listeners. Her song, *Non, Je Ne Regrette Rien,* says it all: I regret nothing,

I don't worry who hears me, I don't worry what they think. When you come from your place of deep energy, your voice expresses fully your excitement, conviction, feeling and sensitivity.

COUNTER-INTUITION

You exercise strong intention and open acceptance at the same time.

RELAX INTO MOVEMENT

Meanwhile, movement or lack of movement in your body also expresses what is going on inside. If your body looks awkward, it's a clear sign that there's awkwardness inside too. If you're anxious, not only is there hindrance to the breath, but also your body becomes tight. When your body is free, your mind is clear. Breathing happens rhythmically and you feel ease of movement reflected in flexible thinking too. You don't feel the need to adjust your deportment to tall and straight; a feeling of openness and energy gives your body good open posture naturally.

Find Your Balance

- Scan through your body now. Where is your centre of gravity? Is it up around your shoulders? If so, stand upright and relaxed, and gently soften your shoulders and knees to settle into a good natural posture.

- Your centre of gravity is then at a point low in your body, just below your tummy button. Turn your attention to this point and imagine your power coming from there. Changing your centre of gravity makes a big difference to your energy and rhythm.
- Now walk forward. Which part of you leads? Is it your head or your chest? If it is, relax, and allow your legs to swing forward easily without any one part of your body forging ahead.

When you let go of tension in your body, it is free to move in every direction and demonstrates grace and economy of movement, and flow coming from your centre. You are balanced and ready for rapid switches from stillness to action and action to stillness. The more relaxed and ready the muscles, the more different ways they can move.

Find Grace in Spontaneous Movement

Preferably standing, but sitting is also fine, just move, gently at first, letting the moment decide spontaneously what that movement will be. Have a sense of following a movement through. Maybe a tiny finger movement gradually creates a turn of the wrist that in turn changes into an arm movement in any direction that feels good. Gradually incorporate more and more of your body into the movement, flowing gracefully from one movement to the next. You might find it enjoyable to accompany this practice with music.

If you are spontaneous, each movement leads with its own volition to the next. It decides for itself without plan or expectation. There's no right or wrong. You just move and enjoy the movement, letting the moment decide without trying to control it.

When you finish, pause for a moment to enjoy what you have just done.

Moshé Feldenkrais, founder of the Feldenkrais Method, talks about reversibility of movement. If you are tense, any movement is awkward and reversing an action quickly is quite impossible. If you are pushing in one direction relentlessly, it is very difficult to reverse your direction suddenly. But when there is no resistance, you can instantly reverse direction. Translate this way of being into your communication, and, quick on your feet, you bring balance, flexibility, responsiveness and flow to your interactions with others.

Andy Murray's Injury

 During the Wimbledon Tennis Championships one year, there was a match in the latter part of which Andy Murray was visibly suffering from a hip injury. This of course affected his speed and flexibility of movement. But it clearly affected his thinking and judgement too, which had an impact on his play more than you could attribute to his physical state alone. Lack of physical balance and wellbeing affected mental and emotional wellbeing too.

When the body is in flow it acts fast at times but always without hurry. Graceful movement is neither fast nor slow; it's as economical as it can effectively be. A rushed response is often a sign that you're out of balance. It results in muscular tension. Mind and body are a single system, so one affects the other.

MOVEMENT REVEALS YOUR INNER PROCESSES

Body movement together with tone of voice provide the broad-brush visible signs of subtle and ever-changing inner energetic activity. What happens inside us is complex. We wouldn't just examine externals to discover how someone drives a car skilfully. Mental, emotional, and inner energy are all vital in our communication.

Flexibility is to the mind what relaxing is to the body. A balanced body in flow is reflected in a balanced mind and intuitive thinking. If you have fixed ideas, change of focus is difficult. But if you are accepting in your mind, you can respond flexibly in conversation to every nuance.

The thinking mind accesses its thoughts through the energy of your whole being and then expresses itself again through the whole body – except when the conduit is blocked and true feeling and good thinking have no means of being expressed. If you are steered by a default agenda, such open responsiveness is impossible. You only have to witness someone assure you quickly that everything is fine, when their whole body is expressing stress and unhappiness, to realise how real communication is blocked by the contradiction of spoken and unspoken messages. If you observe closely someone running an agenda, you will notice a lack of freedom in the body. Maybe breathing is shallow, or shoulders are held slightly high, or their head moves little in relation to shoulders.

Each default agenda has its own typical body pattern, breathing, and way of moving and responding. These holding patterns restrict the person's access to spontaneous feelings of joy, sadness and other basic emotions, and their lack of felt expression inhibits relationships and forfeits trust in conversation.

There's a further huge benefit when your body lets go: it then informs you of deeply embodied insights *before* your mind has become aware of information. Bodily movement precedes words to express the somatic reaction. In conversation with someone, their gestures, tone of voice, micro-movements and breathing often give you information ahead – and at times in direct contradiction – of their words. It's when you let go that you pick up the other person's energy. For example, your body at a cellular level picks up internal conflict or untruthfulness in another person from tiny clues not consciously noticed by your mind, and this awareness is transmitted to the mind at first nonverbally as an instinct or hunch. If you rely solely on your intellectual brain, you miss much of this data and therefore cannot respond accurately or empathetically to the other person.

Listening to Body Wisdom

If you want to be more responsive in conversation, relaxing your body helps you enormously. Freedom in the body releases energy and gives your instinct the chance to serve you well. In its turn, letting go with your mind frees the body in a virtual cycle. The principle applies to all human activity.

- Practise first in an environment where you can observe without being called upon to engage. Maybe there is a meeting or another gathering where you can do that.
- Breathe fully out, without slumping, and release to allow air to fill your lungs. Then breathe normally. Gradually relax fully every part of you, feet, lower legs, knees, thighs, hips, stomach, chest, shoulders, hands and arms, neck, jaw, eyes and forehead.
- As other people contribute to the meeting, be aware of your somatic responses. Which parts of your body are you are most aware of? What bodily sensations do you feel in those parts?
- When you become aware of a particular part of your body, get curious about what it is telling you regarding the situation.

3

BE SPONTANEOUS
IN THE MOMENT

> *You might think this is about a joyful future, but*
> *It is about your actual and present experience,*
> *the here and now, your cash in hand.*
> – Rumi

You are attentive in the here and now, dancing spontaneously in the moment. Rather than consciously 'noticing' and 'focusing' you are awake to what is actually there in front of you, without your usual preconceptions, assumptions, and internal chatter. This quality of attention, characteristic of right-brain thinking, radically affects the outcome of your conversation.

Be in the Now

'Your actual and present experience, the here and now', says Rumi. This moment right now is vividly alive and you are vividly alive living it. Except when you're not.

What is this 'here and now'? Whatever the reason for your communication, it will go best if you are an alert presence, truly in the moment without distraction. Being in the now at its most basic is about being physically present. That means having your five senses awake and available externally. Your eyes focus outwards, your ears hear whatever is physically audible, and your sense of touch/feeling is sensitive to what is happening on the outside in the present moment. You focus externally, without losing consciousness of your own inner state.

Detach from Past and Future

One obvious but critical feature of present attention is the absence of past and future. As R. S. Thomas writes in his beautiful poem *The Bright Field*, 'Life is not hurrying| on to a receding future, nor hankering after| an imagined past'. Life is to be found in a brief ephemeral moment of beauty. That is our eternity. Everything happens *now*. The past is past and the future never comes: when it comes, it's now. Opportunity arises in the now. And yet this is an unusual state for humans to remain in for more than a few moments at a time. We constantly escape to past or future in our minds, and in those moments we lose our awareness of the information-full, vibrating here and now.

Just pause in your reading and sit quietly for a few moments. Catch any thought – it's probably looking forward or back. Don't worry: it's the same for all of us. Now come into the present for a moment, here in this place, sitting or standing like this, with these sounds around you and these feelings in your body, and this breathing … here … now.

Many people when they chat spend most of the time they're not talking thinking about what they're going to say next. Others compare what you've just said with their own stories. Either way, they're absent. Even skilful communicators often find their first instinct is to consider their store of knowledge, their past experience, or to think about a goal, the future. As soon as you judge, assess, or have an agenda, you have lost presence.

In communication we constantly refer to our bank of knowledge built up over the years. But conversation depends crucially on our ability to respond using our intelligence *in the moment,* reading the situation holistically in the here and now – a powerful right-brain mode of attention.

Being fully present enables you to respond lightly and quickly to events as they evolve. Responding in the present moment is very different to a knee-jerk reaction to events. You can't respond to something you haven't expected unless you're present and aware. Presence is the soil in which communication can blossom. Conversation happens in the now. You can plan and prepare, but anything may happen. The more aware you can be of what is actually present now, the more likely you are to find the right thing to say in the right way at the right time, without even consciously thinking about it. Earnest Hemingway suggested that to be fully in the moment was to 'open yourself to the powerful energies dancing around you', which describes it beautifully, I think.

TIME AND SPACE

The present seems like no time, merely the infinitesimal gap between past and future. Yet paradoxically time is *always* the now, so in a sense the present continues forever. This present moment, this *now,* has time and space. It is not hurried or urgent. You have all the time you need, a rightness of time, without tension. You are in this present moment, not detached from it, but you also have ample space to breathe. Out of this spacious breath comes the appropriate thought, the right thing to say.

People who practise the martial arts recognise this state of presence. The master is quiet and still, knowing that an attack can come from anywhere. And when it comes the speed of the attack dictates the move. The master is lightly ready in the moment and responds in lightning time with grace and flow. He or she achieves this by being quiet in body and mind, and balanced and light on the feet.

When you are fully present the energy of your life force is able to find expression. Coleman Barks, who spent a lifetime creating poetic versions of Rumi's poems from other English translations, suggests that good scientists and mystics, chefs and surgeons, historians and athletes all share a lovingly careful wonder, 'the nail head of attention and spontaneity', that allows insights to emerge. In that moment, you experience the sparkling ecstasy of the living moment and become light and full of joy.

No Fixed Plan

 The celebrated conductor Bruno Walter explained that although an orchestral conductor follows a written score and in one sense knows exactly what is going to happen in any piece of music, he also interacts closely in the present moment with his players. He has to know his players moment by moment and go with their flow, not just with his own fixed plan. Players and conductor interact with each other to create music in the moment, just like a conversation.

Martin Luther King, speaking to a huge crowd of supporters on the steps of the Lincoln Memorial in Washington DC on a famous day in 1963, suddenly abandoned his prepared speech halfway through to exclaim 'I have a dream', and speak about his hopes for the future of the United States. This spontaneous part of his speech has gone down in history as one of the most influential orations ever made.

Actor Claire Foy, who played Queen Elizabeth in the film *The Crown,* told interviewer Tom Lamont that the most important thing she learned to do as an actor was 'not to try to pre-empt everything – to stay in the moment'.

In conversation, no plan can guarantee the response of the other person. If you do stick rigidly to a plan, you forfeit the possibility of a generative process emerging. An authentic conversation depends on the spontaneity of both speakers in their interaction with each other.

When, through understandable caution in your dealings with the world, you exclude spontaneity, you lose the power of the moment. This happens more often than you'd hope in a business context where over-caution causes people to smother their genuine reactions. Sometimes, I suspect that spontaneous laughter would be more effective than yet more wordy admiration of the Emperor's new clothes.

DANCING IN THE MOMENT

Executive and life coaches sometimes talk about dancing in the moment with their clients. It's an interesting metaphor; you might think a steady, reassuring presence might be recommended. But it reflects the reality that relating to people requires constant shifts, rebalancing and flexibility, even the ability at times to 'bounce back' with resilience.

Solutions arise beyond consciousness in the safety and creativity of a relationship. Too much focus on desired goals can trap people forever in a never-arriving future, despite positive intent. Strong focus on evidence of the past can too easily produce reasons without present progress. When holding the space in the dancing present, intelligence emerges spontaneously in the here and now, neither thought out nor thought through, but exquisitely calibrated to the issue in hand.

Pay Exquisite Attention

COUNTER-INTUITION

Pay forensic attention AND just absorb the moment.

AWARENESS AND THINKING ARE NOT THE SAME THING

In the most satisfying conversations both participants are paying attention. It is simple to pay attention: simple, but not easy. What are you doing when you pay exquisite attention? You are seeing with your eyes, hearing with your ears, and feeling with your sense of touch. Your senses of smell and taste are also alive. You are awake and aware, while accepting of what is happening – active, yet passive.

What are you NOT doing when you are fully aware? You are not thinking *about* something. When you do that, you immediately find yourself assessing, describing, defining, comparing, conceptualising, quantifying, analysing, judging, interpreting, deciding, defending, cataloguing or concluding. You might *think* you are listening, because you are taking in information from the other person, but in the moments in which you are engaged with any or all of those extra processes, you are no longer attending because you are no longer aware of *what is*. For those periods of thinking *about*, you are no longer witness to the present moment. Thinking and attending don't happen at the same time.

When you practise being awake, you become aware of just how much our lives are lived on the automatic pilot of thinking, not attending. Time and again we miss moments of wonder and awareness through inner chatter or emotions such as anxiety.

Missing the Moment to Catch the Moment

 It is tremendously easy to slip from attending into thinking and recording. When the Olympic cycle race passed through my town of Dorking, I was determined to witness the special event. I found the perfect location to watch the race and kept my eyes on the road in eager anticipation of catching the leading cyclists as they passed. Spotting them as dots in the distance, I grabbed my smart phone. I took the all-important photograph; but I missed the race. By the time I looked up from the aperture the cyclists had already zoomed past me.

I was struck by another striking smart phone example when I visited the Rijksmuseum in Amsterdam this year.

The crowds were thick in front of the famous huge Rembrandt picture, *The Night Watchman*, and I wasn't surprised that many were looking into the screens of their phones to get the perfect picture. But many also were facing away from the picture and were busy taking selfies of themselves with the Rembrandt as their backdrop – not looking at the picture at all!

We also miss the moment by the simplest action of naming an experience in the midst of experiencing it. For example, you hear the sound of a thrush singing in the early evening and you are enchanted. You comment to yourself, 'Oh that's a thrush, what a wonderful sound; ah, there it is at the top of the fir tree over there', and as soon as you do that, you are no longer experiencing but 'making sense of' and the quality of the experience changes.

When you are present for another person, you are not concentrating hard but you are exquisitely aware. You listen and notice best when you have a soft focus. This is something a cat knows how to do. It has a state of alertness where it stays perfectly still, yet active. Every cell of its body is alive, from its whiskers to the tip of its tail, watching, listening, and sensing, ready to make a move if the right moment comes.

COUNTER-INTUITION

When you relax and soften your focus, your attention becomes more acute.

It's a right-brain skill. Whereas the left hemisphere of the brain knows in advance the kind of data it is looking for and focuses on relevant details, the right hemisphere maintains a sustained awareness without any preconception or agenda, awake to whatever might transpire.

Hearing and Seeing Accurately

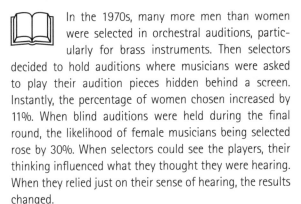

In the 1970s, many more men than women were selected in orchestral auditions, particularly for brass instruments. Then selectors decided to hold auditions where musicians were asked to play their audition pieces hidden behind a screen. Instantly, the percentage of women chosen increased by 11%. When blind auditions were held during the final round, the likelihood of female musicians being selected rose by 30%. When selectors could see the players, their thinking influenced what they thought they were hearing. When they relied just on their sense of hearing, the results changed.

Something similar happens when an amateur artist attempts to draw a still life. The proportions come out wrong because the artist's left-brain *knows* too much a priori about the shapes of objects – oranges are round, a tray is square, and so on. Then his teacher tells him to draw the spaces in and around the objects, and not having any pre-knowledge of the shapes of these negative spaces, he creates a drawing that's more accurate and realistic.

SEEING THINGS AFRESH

While the left-brain searches for evidence to make a case and mostly spots what it expects to see, the right-brain suspends judgement and fully accepts whatever it attends to. The right-brain knows that it's more important to catch the particular shade of a shadow on a wall than to revisit your knowledge of the situation from past experience.

Always New

 In the months before my father died, he became repetitive in his speech, and when I saw him, I sometimes felt impatient with his comments that I'd heard so many times before. Now, I realise that through interpreting the situation I wasn't hearing him properly. When, for example, he said, 'I walked up the road to the gate today – I go for a walk every day you know', he was just repeating a well-worn refrain as far as I was concerned. But I now think that as his strength gradually deserted him, he was telling me about a personal victory that was fresh for him as it got harder and harder day by day. I now want to congratulate him. 'Wow, was that very hard today, Dad, when your strength had deserted you? What a splendid victory to get all the way there, *today*!'

When you are fully awake and attend closely, nothing is already known; everything is fresh and new.

Seeing with New Eyes

 The guitarist Wilko Johnson, after being informed that he had terminal cancer, visited a beautiful temple in Kyoto in Japan and saw everything with new eyes. Where normally he would have been trying to process the scene as a *memory* so that he could refer to it in the future, this time, believing his days to be numbered and seeing no point in creating a memory, he experienced the scene completely in the moment and it was sublime.

Marcel Proust suggested that the real voyage of discovery consists not in seeking new lands but in seeing with new eyes. Perhaps you have had the experience of returning after many years to a place that was once familiar, and in that first moment of return, although little has changed, everything is new and unknown – you see the scene afresh, with today's eyes, and in that moment you know much that was hidden from you before.

There's a well-known saying by the Greek philosopher Heraclitus: 'No man ever steps in the same river twice, for it's not the same river and he's not the same man.' There's a comfort in accepting this statement, an absence of expectation and a release from pretence. What happens today is what happens today. Nothing is fixed or inevitable. It's only the left-brain that insists on consistency. My communication today is the communication of today, the way it is, not the same as yesterday and not the same as tomorrow, just this way, today's way. That's a useful thought to take into your next daunting presentation too.

HOLDING ON TO CURIOSITY

Soft focus is a good companion for gentle curiosity. I have a desire to know you better, a desire that's unwilling to jump to easy conclusions. My inner reflection is likely to be, 'That's interesting …' rather than, 'So that means …'. I intuit that the longer I delay in deciding I know all about you, the more fruitful our time together will be.

When I'm curious, I have no idea what I am going to find. I'm not like a research scientist who looks for the precise faulty gene that causes a particular defect, keeping a narrow focus on what she is looking for. My curiosity is more like vigilance; I stay awake to *whatever* might be there, without any preconception. Moreover, I am open to possibility as regards meaning, quite prepared for uncertainty or confusion, not insistent on grasping the explicit significance of what I find.

How to Be in the Now

Many different practices can help you to be more present. Here are a few ideas.

Use your Peripheral Vision to Absorb the Whole

- Sit or stand comfortably and keep your head upright and still, facing forwards.
- Now, without moving your head, extend your attention out to each side to bring into your awareness what is on either side of you equally, while maintaining gentle awareness of what is

ahead of you as well. Gently absorb without locking onto anything. Keep your eyes soft, breathe and don't strain.

Enjoy the experience of absorbing the big picture. You'll find that different particulars come into your awareness, an acute sense of movement, for example. You'll also find that in this state you are aware of the whole of your visual field and can respond instantly to anything.

Tune Up Your Five Senses

Cultivate all your senses, including smell and taste.

- Go for a gentle meander with all five senses attuned and just allow the merest hint of desire, aversion, or hunch to tell you which way to go and when to pause for a while.
- Experiment with each of your senses separately:
  - listen for a while
  - watch for a while
  - be aware of external touch and feelings in your body for a while
  - experiment also with the senses of smell and taste.

You'll probably find that you use one or two senses more than others. Nurture all five senses at different times if you can, and practise especially with those you usually exercise least. Find pleasure in noticing more than you usually do. Avoid making meaning or telling yourself stories about what you notice.

Practise Mindfulness

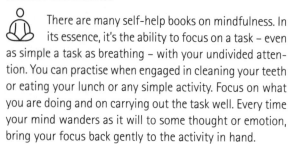 There are many self-help books on mindfulness. In its essence, it's the ability to focus on a task – even as simple a task as breathing – with your undivided attention. You can practise when engaged in cleaning your teeth or eating your lunch or any simple activity. Focus on what you are doing and on carrying out the task well. Every time your mind wanders as it will to some thought or emotion, bring your focus back gently to the activity in hand.

This practice can be as simple as switching off for a while. This is hardly a practice, more a non-practice. We all need time to do nothing – as Winnie the Pooh so perceptively put it, 'just going along, listening to all the things you can't hear, and not bothering'. Give yourself this time, without anxiety, impatience, or feeling you should be doing something more useful. Like Turner, gaze at the clouds in the sky, or look at the cracks in the pavement or the steam rising from your cup of tea. When gremlin thoughts pop up, relax, let the gremlins drift off, just *be* for a while.

Try any of these ideas, and you'll notice over time how you feel calmer and more present.

Deep Listening

Being in the moment opens up the possibility of listening well. We think we listen, but much of the time we don't, not really. When we react to familiar signals in a conversation and answer by default, we're not listening; we're hearing what we already know inside our head. And – surprise, surprise – in so doing we just confirm what we already know.

Talking to a good friend one day, she asked me how I was. I felt that she really only wanted to hear good news when I wanted to tell her about a sadness in my life, so I wasn't fully available to listen to *her*. We were like ships passing in the night. If your head is full, you cannot listen. You can listen only when you are fully available for the other person, and that's possible only if your energy isn't taken up with your own issues, performance anxiety or self-consciousness.

COUNTER-INTUITION

Your self actually grows and expands when not obsessed *with* itself.

Listen. Just listen. Be. Just *be* there. Listen to the sounds of the room, the air in the room, the atmosphere in the room. Listen with your heart and gut, with your spine and the hairs on the back of your neck. Listen with every cell in your body. But listen without straining. Listening is to absorb everything in your field. When you listen like that, your whole intelligence comes into play. Franz Kafka reminds us there's nothing to be done but to become quiet and still, and then the world 'will roll in ecstasy at your feet'.

You can sense when someone is really listening to you. For me it's an alive, buzzy feeling: it might be different for you. And when someone is not really listening, at some level you're aware of the lack of connection. This has little to do with their responses, and everything to do with the quality of their attention – on how they *are* more than what they *do*.

When you attend with open focus, you get a different result from times when you listen in order to achieve something, such as to give assistance or gain information or behave socially. One listening is a listening for data: what happened, who did what, what are the relevant details? With this kind of awareness, you are listening *in order to* ... find a response, do something, or achieve something. Even listening in order to reply rather than to understand comes into this first category. This kind of listening uses our personal data bank of reference and personal experience.

'Data listening' makes patterns, like plotting everything the other person is saying onto a map. So, for example, a story about something that happened in the office may get plotted in the listener's brain as a story about unfairness. The listener thinks, 'This story is an example of that', and then gives to the listening task whatever he knows about the subject of unfairness. Someone talks about some personal pain in their marriage, and the other person responds, albeit with sympathy, that marriage can be fraught with difficulty after a certain number of years. Whatever is unique to the storyteller is missed in generalisation and standard responses and remedies.

The other listening is to attend without preconceptions or expec-tations. You hear not only what the person is saying but also what they are *not* saying. You register silence, tone of voice, simile and metaphor, irony and humour. With this kind of exquisite listening, you actually change the quality of the other person's thinking.

You're present to the newness of this unique situation; you cannot move rapidly on to certainties because there are none.

Here there is more accurate listening with deep empathy, unique to the moment. It's embedded in relationship. This kind of listening can get to the heart of sticky problems. This kind of listening – even without saying a word – can bring about resolution and healing.

Iain McGilchrist suggests that not only do you get a different result when you listen with open attention, but that the kind of attention you bring to bear changes the nature of the world you attend to. We each create our world by what we notice. In conversation, in how you both attend, you are both changed by the experience.

COUNTER-INTUITION

Thinking less, you know more.

4

BE WHOLEHEARTED

> *Naught but Love itself*
> *can explain love and lovers!*
> *None but the sun*
> *can display the sun.*
> – Rumi

When you embrace your energy and go all-out to follow what you love, you communicate at a higher frequency that inspires and energises. True insight emerges when you keep your mind open in the uncertainty of 'not-knowing', instead of assuming you already know what people are like. You neither push solutions, nor force an analytical approach, but connect with trust. This means having the courage to be vulnerable.

The Real 100%

When you get in touch with your life force, you experience more than physical and mental energy. For when your energy is not blocked by agendas or inhibitions and your body and mind release, your *heart* is free to be whole. You get in touch with your *love* force and this gives you more subtle resources for responding to people.

Life Force in Sport

 I had the pleasure of watching the tennis player Laura Robson play a singles match at Wimbledon when she was 16 years old. In someone so young, it was particularly easy to perceive the difference between playing a shot energetically and excellently, as she had been coached to do, and giving it the full 100% – as she did three times with a match point against her. At those fearful moments of potentially losing the match, she threw her absolute all into the moment with searing cross-court shots that astounded the crowd.

You would call playing a shot excellently 100% if you didn't have the real 100% with which to compare it. When you do compare, the difference is huge. In the first you witness well-executed preparation, signs of forethought, and excellent technical execution – you see someone doing all the *right things*. But in the second you are in the presence of intense relaxed concentration, deep breathing, and extraordinary power, focus and follow-through. The second example declares silently that there is *no way* this point is going to be lost – and we all feel it. Nothing seems calculated; the shot seems a spontaneous expression of an inner life-affirming power. It's not doing the *right* thing; it's going all the way for its own sake, for the joy of bringing 100% to it. It says, 'All or nothing at this point, and I choose *all*!'

If we are spectators to such play, we feel the excitement of witnessing someone intensely in the now; we sense the physical wellbeing and enjoyment, creativity and powerful intention. And it energises us in the most exhilarating way.

COUNTER-INTUITION

You are 100% emotional available AND 100% mentally alert.

If you enjoy driving, you may sometimes experience an in-the-moment feeling of power and confidence on the road. One kind of driving consists of obeying traffic rules – speed limits, double white lines, traffic lights, and so on. Your attention is on doing it right according to the regulations and it seldom energises you. On other roads there's the possibility of driving *well* – choosing your speed and road position according to the weather, road conditions, curves in the road, and your awareness of potential hazards, enjoying fluidity of acceleration and deceleration and car handling. I'm not talking particularly about driving fast; it's about freedom in performance, and good drivers find such driving energising and enjoyable.

Driving safely and well brings in the attention of your right-brain, whereas obeying road instructions is a left-brain process. Driving well is about responding moment by moment to rapidly changing conditions and information. When we use that part of our brain, we hone our skills. Obeying traffic signs, we learn no such lessons; indeed, we maybe habituate ourselves to *not* using our spontaneous awareness. The growing numbers of road instructions prove their worth in a left-brain world by improving death and injury statistics, but they are not turning us into more skilful drivers – maybe actually the reverse.

Sometimes an ambitious leader learns a speech by heart, even factoring in emphasis and expression, and his audience is impressed. But though he may achieve perfection through remembering the speech verbatim in terms of accuracy, tone and body language, heartfelt spontaneity is missing and discerning members of the audience can feel its absence. As long as you are aware that a performance is a performance – however brilliant – there's a gap in communication. You're not quite there. Great actors know this truth. If you concentrate on learning performance skills alone, you learn to perform; but that's not the whole story, you need to connect – to touch – as well. Every communication truly from the heart holds far more complexity than such planned displays – and connects more directly and authentically with people.

The contrast between doing something correctly and doing it wholeheartedly is as stark as the difference between painting by numbers and creating a masterpiece. You might not be able to *describe* the difference in simple terms, but you can certainly *sense* it. Just as you can sense clearly the difference between a politician who asks herself the question, 'What does it mean to be a great politician?' (and lives by the answer), and one who asks herself, 'What steps do I have to take to remain in power?'

QUALITIES OF WHOLEHEARTEDNESS

I've used several different images to demonstrate the difference between performing something well and doing it wholeheartedly. It's a difference that's not easy to measure. However, you won't mistake the feeling of wholeheartedness at times when you are intensely and pleasurably focused on something so completely that there is simply no space for self-consciousness or thinking *about* or concern. Some people find dangerous sports exhilarating and energising for this reason. If you are clinging to the side of a mountain with a huge drop beneath you, there just isn't attention to spare for worrying about your performance – every part of you is engaged in the exhilarating moment.

How does wholeheartedness manifest itself in conversation? When you engage with someone who is wholehearted, they are 100% available to you. All their tiny sensitive nerve end-ings, invisible in crude everyday exchange, are tuned to you. Their words touch you viscerally. You receive their attention, their energy, and their empathy without agendas and without reserve – they are fully present.

When you are wholehearted yourself, you no longer rely solely on your intelligence to know what to say and when to keep silent. Instead, you trust your whole mind that includes your gut feeling and heart's intuition. These offer a larger perspective; not exclud-ing your intellect but going beyond.

If you're talking to someone and have the clear intuition to say something, and then part of you pulls back and you fail to speak for fear of how they'll take it, you lose your power. If there's a gap between who you think yourself to be and the words you say or the way you relate to others, you're out of alignment and it's harder for your listeners to connect with you. This divided, *half-hearted*, state is tiring. Mind, body, heart, and spirit need to work together, the real you being the same as the person you present to the world. If you *do* manage to speak in this situation, even when fear is present, the result is a surge of energy. Being authentic, you find your power.

Voice tone, non-verbal language and words are all elements of the same story. You're willing for others to see you as you are. This removes the need to hide parts of yourself and allows you to tap into your deeper intuition. In that state of mind, you tune in to everything that is going on, and others find it easy to trust you. That's wholeheartedness.

Be Happy to Not-Know

You might think that lack of certainty would be another factor to pull you in different directions. But in fact, not knowing or feeling confused is not something to avoid. When humans interact with each other, sometimes there *is* confusion. If fear and uncertainty cause you instantly to leap in to take control and rush head-long into answers, you close down possibility and often make bad judgements.

But if you stay open and allow any feelings of confusion or discomfort to be present, without being tempted to escape into a quick reaction or a diversionary tactic, then a better answer emerges naturally from your intuition. Wisdom arises when the usual blocks of control, inhibition, roles, others' opinions and – above all – fear no longer inhibit you.

An ability to live with uncertainty lies at the core of intuitive thinking and underpins every worthwhile conversation. It's the bubbling melting pot in which ideas are broken down to allow something new to be formed. Many creative people comment on its importance. The poet John Keats suggested it was the mark of a great thinker to be 'capable of being in uncertainties, mysteries, doubts, without any irritable reaching after fact and reason'. He called it a 'negative capability'. The artist Edgar Degas claimed that a painter only did good things when he no longer knew what he was doing. The writer Michael Gelb calls confusion 'the welcome mat at the door of creativity'.

Instead of confusion, one might use the term *openness to uncertainty*. You remain open in the space of unknowing long enough for something to pop up from the right hemisphere of your brain, instead of depending on the already known. For many of us, this skill is something we un-learned very thoroughly in formal education, with its emphasis on the acquisition of knowledge and repetition of known facts. It's not just not-knowing, but being *content* with uncertainty, okay with paradox, open to possibility, aware that at the same place in the river we are never in the same water. Sell your cleverness and buy bewilderment, says Rumi. Sometimes 'I don't know' is the most powerful statement you can make.

Leaving the Door Ajar

 Nobel Prize winner, physicist Richard Feynman, considered one of the best scientific minds since Albert Einstein, confided in a BBC *Horizon* interview that he was content to live with doubt and uncertainty and not knowing. He thought it was more interesting to live not knowing than to have answers that might be wrong, and that it was important for scientists 'to leave the door to the unknown ajar'.

Let's think about how uncertainty arises in conversation. Imagine two people talking and the conversation falters. One person does not know what to say next, but he refrains from controlling his response and stays with that uncertainty without resorting to past patterns or agendas. Even as the situation starts to mirror past awkwardness, he stays present and aware in a space where he trusts not only himself but also the other person and the situation. He 'holds the space' and holds the silence too until words emerge, uncalculated, unanticipated, fresh, and true. There is nothing else for him to do in this situation but to get out of his own way by keeping open the doors of perception and staying alive to possibility. The words after the pause are often important ones that open up something new and different.

When you're wholehearted, you allow yourself to be spontaneous, authentic and free from striving; and you give yourself deep permission to say anything, free from control. Deepak Chopra talks about the 'wisdom of uncertainty'. If you're unable to live with uncertainty, the feeling turns to fear. When you accept uncertainty, insecurity vanishes, and so you're free.

Holding Back

 One day, a client was telling me about a sensitive subject, and at a certain point I was uncertain whether he was talking about his wife or his work group. Had I missed a connection, or was it he who had become confused? I was tempted to interrupt and clarify the point for myself; but then I reflected that I didn't need to know. Maybe in a sense he was talking about both, and a focused question would break the moment?

I breathed and continued to listen. And so it transpired; he realised a short while later that his different stories were all being carried on the back of a particular emotion, which was the core of his problem. My holding back allowed the right side of his brain space to give him emotional information invisible to the rational part of his brain and find his own solution.

BOTH/AND

As described earlier, most conversations on TV and radio news are set up as interchanges between people with opposing points of view, with the interviewer intent on keeping the argument polarised. This keeps the conversation simple and controllable, but usually prevents anything interesting or unexpected from developing. Control can only hold a view that excludes its opposite. It can lead me to talk with only my own interest at heart, and therefore deprive you of yours; or to assert that I'm right and therefore know that you're wrong; or to speak 'for your own good' rather than work with you. Control in its lack of flexibility tends to *create* opposition.

An acceptance of uncertainty allows us to adopt more subtle positions, such as the paradox of holding opposing perspectives as both true or recognising the feasibility of synergy between differing arguments. In conversation, 'either/or' will give you one kind of exchange; 'both/and' will give you another more interesting and surprising encounter. What if I'm right *and* you're right? The mind has to stretch to something radically different to cope with such a thought.

The concept applies also to my thoughts about you. Adopting an either/or attitude, if I have the thought that you are selfish, my left-brain will come up with various bits of information to confirm my thought. I'll decide that you are selfish *because:* because you forgot an important appointment; because you grabbed a work opportunity that everyone wanted; because you never thanked me for help I'd given you – I compile a mental list. But with that same thought that you are selfish, I could develop my thinking in a different way. I could continue my thought with 'and also': you were selfish today, and also you showed generosity on other occasions; or I've witnessed you being selfish *and* I've also seen how much you care for your children. The latter way will give me less cut and dried certainty but will offer me a richer portrait of you and maybe an opening to new thinking.

The synthesis of opposites is a powerful force in communication. When you talk with someone, you may want to be highly ener-gised *and* relaxed, or to act with daring *and* with humility; you may want to engage with playfulness *and* seriousness, or inno-cence *and* experience – both at the same time.

Opening to Flow

Our best communication is largely an unconscious proposi-tion – something that flows from deep within us. Being in flow feels like not knowing exactly what we are doing but being quietly confident that whatever it is, it's okay. The pianist Claudio Arrau said he never knew what was going to happen in a concert but also knew it was going to be something wonderful. Don't be concerned that you might confuse this state with reckless confidence. The feeling is distinctly different.

Flow is never present in conversation where there is self-consciousness, excessive control or structure, judgement, or rigid insistence on particular outcomes. Negative states are equally harmful. Self-criticism is deadly. You might be aware of times when you are in a negative mood and nothing goes right; maybe you even drop things or trip up because you are out of balance. I remember once making a long drive home halfway through a two-day conference, already self-critical, sure that the better decision would have been to spend the evening meeting people and to stay the night. I drove into our drive as I had done hundreds of times and caught a brick wall with the side of the car, something I couldn't have dreamed of ever doing before. My brain, and therefore coordination, was definitely out of flow.

When you become defensive, blame others, and don't accept and surrender to the moment, your life meets resistance. In coaching, dancing in the moment means to dance to the tune of the client but like a jazz player, remembering not to leave your own creativity at home. In conversation, too, it's a two-way process where the input of the other person actually stimulates your own creativity and the energy flows between you, to and fro.

A good way to move towards flow is to act *as if* you already have the mastery you are seeking. Nelson Mandela treated his guards in prison *as if* they were worthy of his respect, and by so doing achieved their respect. Set your intention. Act *as if* your intuition is to be trusted. Act *as if* you are already in flow.

What are the ideal conditions for a state of flow? Enjoyment certainly – often the enjoyment of a challenge that's just within your power to achieve. Enjoyment encourages iteration and practice becomes a pleasure. Enjoyment turns everything into play and progress becomes effortless. You find you are pursuing excellence for its own sake rather than for admiration or personal gain. Enjoyment promotes focus. Energy and clarity in the moment are created when there's space – space to breathe, space for humour: a few moments to gaze up at the stars and – like the extraordinary dung beetle that is guided by the Milky Way! – find your true direction.

WAYS TO NURTURE FLOW

If you enjoy talking and listening to people, you'll become good at it. Realise that conversation in depth is not an intellectual exercise, like a sport, but a *connection*. Learn to recognise the beautiful clarity and energy you experience when it just happens. Get to know the playful free state of mind that allows it to happen. Trust it.

When musicians at the height of their powers practise, they don't just repeat sections by rote. Instead, they bring heart and soul-awareness to their practice. They feel confident enough to risk curiosity, wonder and spontaneous delight, even when they are grappling with technical difficulties. Listen to a master practise a phrase: it never sounds the same two times running; creativity is still alive even for technical issues. This is a useful mode of working for any of us. Whatever you practise, practise in a heartfelt way – even if it's an everyday task, bring your heart to it as well as your head. Explore the task with a 'new mind'; feel your way to new possibilities. Never postpone enjoyment until this particular task is finished: savour this moment; enjoy the expression of *this* activity.

You may like to revisit the High Energy and Deep Relaxation practice in the *Become an Awakener* chapter (Chapter 2). Energy and relaxation come together at the same time to produce the experience of flow.

Trust the Heart – Allow Vulnerability

Miracles happen in conversation when you give your whole being to the exchange without fear of the outcome. Everyone wants to be validated and understood, and this becomes possible when the other person opens their heart to you and invites you in. It's more than attention. The poet Mary Oliver wrote of an important lesson she learned from her life partner, that our attention to others only counts if it exists together with openness or empathy and feeling.

We can, of course, connect with each other on an intellectual level through mutual pursuits or ideas that interest us both, but the chief connector, even in these cases, is almost always our love for the pursuit, which brings us back to the heart. And the part of our body we most fear to break is the heart. W. B. Yeats entreats his reader, 'Tread softly because you tread on my dreams'.

We often want to look our best with others and, in order to appear better than we feel we actually are, we put on a mask of competence, confidence or charm. But however impressive, a mask is just that – a mask – and in putting it on, our true self becomes invisible to the other person. The only way to reach them is through transparency, and that can be scary. It means learning to trust.

Trust is the foundation stone of connection and it's generated, not through rationality, but through wholeheartedness. Carl Jung used to urge his students to learn their theories well but put them aside when they touched 'the miracle of the living soul'.

There's no way to create trust through generalised attitudes in communication; it's always personal. With trust, your body softens, your voice loses tension and becomes more harmonious, your eyes and features become more alive, and your listening more empathetic. The other person responds by feeling recognised and acknowledged.

We can control our rationality, but our heart often feels as if it has a will of its own, and we are never quite prepared for its sudden palpitations. Our left-brain would like to pin down trust, but it can no sooner be controlled than the wind. We just feel it personally or interpersonally and decide it. We have fragile confidence without proof.

How can most of us reach the point of feeling safe enough to trust when we engage with other people? Safety is often connected with having control of your environment, but control in conversation doesn't make us safer; rather, it divides us from each other. If, on the other hand, we leave the door to our inner-self open a chink, we encourage others to come closer and dispel their fear. In opening the door, we make ourselves vulnerable, but vulnerability opens others' hearts. When you allow yourself to be vulnerable to another human being you have the chance to touch the beautiful essence of each other beyond games and poses and roles and agendas. It doesn't matter if you tremble, stutter or shake: your opening to another gives them courage and builds your own confidence. It *is* a letting go, so there's risk. You step off the edge of the cliff with nothing to hold on to, trusting you'll fly.

Showing vulnerability doesn't mean hanging out your dirty washing or displaying unfettered emotions. You've probably met people who over-share and it doesn't make for closeness. It's rather allowing yourself to be seen without trying too hard to hide the bits you suspect might not be approved of. It's that moment when you tell someone that you love them before you have confirmation that they love you, or you dare to name something that has not yet been named. This is quite in keeping with the counter-intuitive nature of whole-mind conversation: what feels like a weakness is in fact a strong and courageous act. Gareth Malone who presented the BBC2 show, *The Choir,* expressed the paradox well when he said: 'It takes a certain amount of strength to reach your vulnerability in singing.'

When we communicate professionally with people, instead of relying on our usual dependable skills and strategies, we could find our safety in remaining vulnerable and communicating without knowing where the conversation will take us. It might take courage, but as Brene Brown confirms in her popular Ted Talk on vulnerability, we try to protect ourselves through control, but vulnerability is actually where our power lies as well as our hurt.

COUNTER-INTUITION

In your vulnerability you find your safety and power.

People speak quite often about the importance of trust in business relationships. Neuroscience shows us that's it's even more important than we thought. Psychologists Lane Beckes and James A. Coan have demonstrated that in challenging situations we function far better and with less stress if someone we trust is near, even if there's nothing they can do about the situation. When we are with someone we trust, we have more neural resources for thinking, creating and exploring and are more likely to maintain our health. Businesses with a confrontational competitive culture might find this research particularly useful.

Trusting always holds within it a willingness to let go and risk loss. While you hold on to a situation – maybe a relationship that's not working or a job that doesn't use your talents – you cannot employ heartfelt thinking. Only when you allow for the possibility of hurt and loss are you able to see what really needs to be done. Feel your inner strength as you allow yourself to take a risk. Remember that the word 'courage' comes from the root word 'coeur' or 'heart'. Find your heart.

Trust thrives when we have the courage to live in the heart. The unexpected awaits us at every turn but the heart has energy and wisdom to deal with it. This is not to exclude the intelligence of the head, but to acknowledge that things work best when the heart is leader. We let go of fear and in rushes connection, love, and joy – our wise inner knowing.

Vulnerability and Self-Protection in Music Mastery

 Is there vulnerability in a great musical performance? I think there is, always. Technique, however brilliant is never enough. In his book, *Always Playing*, the violinist Nigel Kennedy points to classical soloists who have superior technique but play 'antiseptically' in order to keep their emotions safe from criticism. He says there is another choice: to express all the emotional elements of the music in a way that connects with your audience, even though that leaves you open and utterly vulnerable to the critics. That is the way he chooses. Kennedy has attracted a lot of controversy in his career for his insistence on individuality, but as the bestselling classical violinist of all time he is hard to ignore.

Michelle Obama and Openness

 Michelle Obama as US First Lady was remarkable for her willingness to reveal her vulnerability. Especially when she was speaking to young people, she would share her own experience and awakening with honesty and compassion and express always her belief in a better future. There was an affirming lack of agenda and absence of ego about her. You sensed her wholeheartedness at every moment. She was one of the most noticed women in the world, yet she had nothing to prove and nobody she had to be. That made her especially powerful as a speaker.

Speaking Through Fear

 Think of a time in communication with someone when you felt that something needed to be said, and in spite of fear you spoke up – and in retrospect realise it was the right thing to have done. Remember your feeling of fear and how that inner courage made you take a breath and speak up despite the fear.

Then remember that good feeling of knowing that it was the right thing for you to have done. *That's* the feeling of being wholehearted.

Practise Trust

Remind yourself frequently to trust yourself, and especially when you are faced with a challenge. Repeat to yourself words of encouragement, such as: 'I am good enough', 'all will be well', 'I don't need to control this, I can ride it instead'. Choose words that mean something to you and strengthen your resolve.

5

CALL FORTH CREATIVITY AND INTUITION

> *You begin as a part of the sun, clouds, and stars,*
> *You rise to be breath, act, word, and thought!*
> – Rumi

When you allow intuition to emerge without stress or forcing, answers pop up spontaneously, ready made and complete from your deep well of holistic intelligence within – creative, generative, and wholly appropriate. You, your ego, disappears and pure consciousness remains.

Imagination and Creativity

There pops into my head the famous rising tune of a song, 'I believe in miracles!' With wholeheartedness the scene is set. Letting go of our conversational defaults and subconscious controls, awakening our life-force energy, paying exquisite attention in the moment, and being wholehearted: all these give space for creativity and invention in our communication with each other. And this is where miraculous things happen.

So, what prompts the miracle – that happy intuition that causes you to say something that lands just right, that small internal prompt to say nothing at a moment when silence is golden? What is the setting and the source that awakens such spontaneous creative wisdom?

When we were very young, and everything was new, our imaginations were free to roam without boundaries. But then we learned customs and systems and rules, and good and bad, right and wrong, taste and tact, seeming and fit, and inappropriate and unsuitable, and our perspective became more limited. The way back to more creative communication is to imagine beyond the confines of our current perception and open ourselves with huge curiosity to see the world afresh.

We cannot achieve this by the normal Western means of conscious industry. We've seen earlier how most of us make an effort to increase our competence and how this effort, trying too hard, easily gets into conflict with feelings of inadequacy such as being too weak or not clever enough. The more our willpower fights such feelings, the more struggle ensues, so that the very effort to be successful sabotages success.

There is a different way, which has a counter-intuitive ring. It's called 'stop trying'.

COUNTER-INTUITION

The best happens when you stop trying.

When you look at extraordinary creative events in art and science, you notice that many of the ideas popped up out of the blue like miracles. Let's examine first the creative process as experienced by artists, musicians and scientists, and then explore its relevance to spontaneous moments in communication.

IDEAS AND INTUITIONS POP UP FULLY FORMED

Creative ideas have always popped up spontaneously, and you wonder where they came from; they seem to well up from absolutely nowhere. This doesn't mean that work is irrelevant, just that work of itself doesn't automatically lead to creativity.

'You ask me where I get my ideas?' demanded Beethoven. 'That I can't say with any certainty. They come un-summoned, directly, indirectly.' 'If I knew where the good songs came from, I'd go there more often', lamented Leonard Cohen.

In science, too, we encounter this phenomenon of ideas just popping up. Einstein imagined chasing after a beam of light and suddenly envisioned relativity. Nicola Tesla had his eureka moment on a walk with a friend when he suddenly stopped to scratch a picture in the earth of how an alternating current would work. Archimedes, Newton – we know the stories.

NON-LINEAR

The creative thought is definitely a leap – a bolt of lightning, jumping the synapses – what Edward de Bono called lateral thinking. Creative ideas don't usually result directly from the linear thinking processes we're most practised in, where thought A is followed by thought B which leads by induction to thought C. On the contrary, the imagination sees invisible connections on different levels simultaneously and an idea is suddenly there in its entirety as an image, a sound, or a feeling.

Time and again, imaginative ideas pop up fully formed, sometimes before being fully understood by the conscious brain. Creativity is not interested in rules and doesn't insist on internal coherence. This is a world where 'both/and' makes perfectly good sense. Like music, which is neither the notes nor the silence between the notes nor even both together, but what *comes about* from the *union* of notes and silence, so creativity cannot be pinned down to particular elements. Each idea is like a gift from heaven, uncalculated, rising suddenly in the consciousness like Rumi's second kind of intelligence, 'the fountain bubbling up from within'. Its working is lightning fast. The *experience* can be of time ceasing to exist or of having all the time in the world to choose the next action.

Being non-linear it's a right-brain activity. Psychologists A. M. Bowden and M. Jung-Beeman showed in experiments how a sudden insight creates a burst of high frequency in the right hemisphere temporal lobe of the brain, preceded by an increase in lower frequency activity over the right posterior cortex.

HAPPENS WHEN YOU'RE LOOKING THE OTHER WAY

It is in the nature of creative thoughts to arrive precisely at a time when we are *not* engaged in the direct task of trying to find an answer. We learn to swim in winter and skate in summer, as Wilhelm Reich remarked. Beethoven answered the question about where his ideas came from by describing their appearance at moments of idleness, out in the open air, in the woods, while walking, in the silence of the night or early in the morning. Archimedes was having a bath. Einstein was daydreaming. It always happened when the conscious mind was given a break.

Sometimes, sudden enlightenment solves a problem different from that being addressed by the conscious mind. The scientist

Spencer Silver discovered the low-tack adhesive we now use as 'post-it' notes when attempting to develop a super-strong adhesive. It suddenly struck him that the weak adhesive he'd actually produced was just what he needed to stop the bookmarker from slipping out of his church hymnbook.

It's common to underestimate the other-than-conscious mind, yet experiments frequently attest to its superiority. In a memory study by Ed Paller and Joel L. Voss, for example, published in *Nature Neuroscience*, subjects were shown a series of abstract images: half of them shown while they were focusing on the task and half when they were deliberately distracted by another task. Then they were shown images again and asked to identify which they had seen before. Their recall was better for images shown while they were being distracted.

SPARKS OF INSPIRATION IN CONVERSATION

COUNTER-INTUITION

You exercise your imagination AND allow insights to arise unprompted.

Sudden insights in conversation are often hard to explain. Your companion suddenly comes out with something that exactly hits the spot. You ask, 'What made you ask that question? Why did you just say what you did?' And the other person replies, 'I don't know. It just came to me. I just got this feeling that it was the right thing to say.'

The creative moment is spontaneous and unsolicited. Analysis and evaluation may follow, but only creative instinct creates the new. It can feel like serendipity. Think of a time when the book that could answer a question deep inside you almost fell out of the shelf into your hands. Remember the time when you met by chance just the person who had the answer for you.

It is remarkably easy to miss some extraordinary insight in conversation by failing to catch a message as it rises in the gap or by quickly vetoing it before even realising what you have done. How many times have I been in that situation! An inspiration can disappear as fast as it came and be irrevocably lost. Presence is everything. Moreover, many times when we fail to follow that inner glimpse of truth, we experience a loss of energy in terms of flatness, emptiness, or lack of direction.

It's when you let go of your idea of how things *should* be, when you take the risk to be open and go with the flow rather than judging and resisting, that you suddenly know how to respond. When both of you are operating from this place in conversation, exciting things can happen.

THE RIGHT SOIL FOR BLOSSOMING

So, how do you learn to come out with the perfect intervention if it just happens involuntarily? Even when you have an inkling of what's going on, how do you *learn* the kind of serendipity artists and scientists talk about?

One thing is certain: inspiration doesn't happen completely in a vacuum. The best creative ideas may seem to strike like lightning with no apparent causal link with what came before, but they are not without foundation, and the richer the foundation, the greater the chance of a lucky strike. The novelist Philip Pullman admits that he doesn't know where the muse comes from but insists it's important to be at your work desk ready for her: 'If you're not there, she goes away again.'

Many times, a period of intensive conscious work is the precursor to a creative breakthrough. For example, the Russian chemist Dmitri Mendeleev invested a huge amount of time in studying the basic elements of the universe but couldn't work out how to arrange them. Then, one night, he fell asleep while chamber music was playing and had a dream in which the basic elements of the universe were flowing together like a piece of music. As soon as he woke up, he wrote down the elements in the order of his dream and created the Periodic Table. Researchers don't always give enough attention to these creative elements of the scientific method!

Sometimes the biggest breakthrough comes when the brain surrenders. It's as if the conscious brain has to say, 'I've given my all. I give up', and hand the baton to the other-than-conscious brain. The scientist Marie Curie woke one morning to find that she had written the answer to a three-year-old problem during the night, after having made the decision the previous day to give up on it altogether.

Creativity in the Air

 The accumulated experience of a lifetime favours good fortune. Matisse did some of his most exciting artwork in old age when, unable to paint any more, he held pieces of coloured paper precariously in the air with one hand and, in glorious extemporisations, cut them freely into shapes with scissors held in the other hand, and then arranged them into collages. The muse was with him in the moment, but his spontaneous instinct rested upon a lifetime of experience, knowledge and skill. In the notes he wrote to accompany an exhibition of a series of his paper cut-out prints entitled *Jazz*, he included the words, 'Obviously, you must have all your experience behind you, and yet know how to keep your instincts fresh'.

Creative Conversation

Translating these ideas into conversation, your solid foundation consists of everything you already understand about human beings and life through listening, watching, and personal experience. Then the moment of serendipity comes when you let go of what you know, stop tapping the conscious mind, and allow the unconscious in. A child uncluttered with fixed prejudices has more chance of it than a knowledgeable but rigid adult.

Serendipity doesn't happen when a procedure is too inflexible, and it often doesn't happen when you're fixed on a specific outcome. The poet Friedrich Schiller said that one function of the creative mind was to withdraw the 'watcher at the gates of the mind' so that ideas can rush in uncontrolled and unexamined – not cut off in their prime by the discriminating and critical left-brain. The moment of creativity comes when the wide-angled right hemisphere of the brain comes into play, open to whatever may be out there. The shift from focus to openness offers the opportunity for surprises to pop up. And they do – but only when the protagonist says yes to what is happening and remains open to whatever may occur. Such openness in communication allows us to be profoundly present to each other and to perceive from different viewpoints at the same time, embracing paradox.

Leaps of Understanding in the Haiku

 The Japanese haiku, a 3-line, 17-syllable form of poem, has been greatly admired and imitated in English. Every genuine haiku performs a leap in the middle from one image to another, and the reader's mind is forced to leap too to make an unexpected connection. It can create a flash of knowing in the reader that is almost impossible to put into words, as suddenly something in the world is revealed in an entirely different light. There's huge delight for both poet and reader in creating or recreating the link.

BEING ENDLESSLY NAIVE AND DELIGHTED AND CURIOUS

There's delight in creativity and creativity is attracted to delight. Rumi remarks in one of his poems that the only intelligent person in the town is the one playing games with children, his wisdom concealed in play. Creativity in play brings huge pleasure – the heart almost bursts with the joy of it. Again, artists and scientists show us the way. The best insights often happen when they are dabbling or experimenting, enjoying serious play away from 'proper' work.

Scientists at Play

 Nobel Prize-winning scientists Andre Geim and Kostya Novoselov often played on Friday nights with new ideas not necessarily linked to their day jobs. They experimented with removing flakes from a lump of bulk graphite (the material of lead in pencils) with everyday sticky tape. By repeatedly peeling off layers from their original flake, they managed to create slivers that were just one atom thick. Their discovery of how to isolate today's most useful material, graphene, came from this out-of-work-hours game.

Musicians find happy serendipities in the art of improvisation, where musical ideas have to emerge in the moment. It was said that Beethoven used to laugh out loud with delight after pouring out his most daring harmonies and melodies in an improvisation. Members of the Bach family loved to extemporise choruses from a mix of popular songs, and would rouse both their audience and themselves to irrepressible laughter. Hear too on YouTube the excitement of players Armen Anassian and Karen Briggs at the end of their spectacular jazz improvisation (https://youtu.be/iL2PZZH5-lo).

In collaborative dramatic improvisation, the creative impulse comes from going *with* what's offered by another player in the game, instead of blocking their input with a 'no'. Players have a direction or an intention in mind, but they don't know how the journey is going to pan out. The process is steered but not held on too tight a rein. If their intention is too rigidly controlled, there is no space for serendipities to occur. In the complete absence of direction, on the other hand, chaos ensues and nothing creative can emerge. Not too tight and not too loose is the mantra. Impro offers good counsel for conversation too.

Theatre, unlike impro, is the art of the repeat performance: actors say the same lines, stand in the same places, and find the same emotional notes. But for the best actors every performance is new, full of minute improvisations within each line that create something original without disturbing the framework of the play. The actor Judi Dench delights in the spontaneity of live performance. She said in interview, 'I think it is always appalling to see yourself on film. I find it too hard to cope with that idea that you can't change it. I love the way in theatre that you can change it every night.' As in child's play, every repetition is different. In changing a performance, you are always learning. 'Always try to find variety,' urged cellist Pablo Casals, 'it is the secret of music.' Life never repeats.

In our daily lives, a conversation is all too often a repetition of many conversations we've had at other times. If our daily words to each other were recorded, many of us would be horrified at the lack of variation. When I ask if you'd like to go out for the evening, and you reply, 'Maybe', I don't need to leap to the meaning I always make of that response which is, 'I knew you wouldn't want to, you never do', but could instead get curious about it. Does 'maybe' express 'maybe yes' as much as 'maybe no'? What would it be like if I acted as if I'd never met you before, instead of jumping to conclusions about meaning? How would a different response from me change the outcome? What if I played this according to the conventions of impro?

How serious must conversation be? Those who don't take others or themselves too seriously get more from it, seriously. In play children enjoy themselves. What if you were to speak with an intention of enjoyment? What if your own words brought you pleasure? What if you experimented with 'making up' answers instead of following the logic of an argument? What if you knew there wasn't such a thing as a mistake?

Happy Mistakes in Science

 When a scientist allows his creativity free rein, a mistake or disaster can be the trigger for a startling revelation. The chance discovery of penicillin through a petri dish culture growth that 'went wrong' is well known. It took a leap of imagination from failure to penicillin; a more rigid mind would have missed the clue in the 'failed' experiment.

An engineer working for Canon thoughtlessly put his soldering iron down on his pen and then, as the pen heated up, ink squirted out of the nib. Instead of annoyance, he leaped to the idea of the inkjet printer.

Viagra was developed to treat patients with angina. When the scientists noticed its famous effect during trials, instead of cursing an unwanted side effect, they envisaged a new use. It is now a hugely popular medication for treating impotence.

Intuition thrives on mistakes and limitations. If an artist finds himself with only chalk and slate, he makes use of what he has, not as a limitation but as an opportunity. In fact, limitation excites the artist's creative mind and provokes fresh ideas. Being given the challenge to fit a poetic idea into 14 lines or a painting into a limited palette helps the unconscious in its creativity.

Exquisite Art from Broken Parts

 The Italian violin-maker Antonio Stradivari created some amazing violins from broken waterlogged oars he found by chance in the docks in Venice. His violins, even now, 300 years later, are considered some of the best ever made and are sold for millions of dollars.

Musicians who improvise use mistakes to create a new pattern or direction. With sound there's no going back, so they make the way forward more exciting and interesting by using what happened by mistake as a purposeful part of their design.

Sculptors are stimulated to use faults in natural marble and wood as essential parts of their creation. The creators of prehistoric cave paintings at Lascaux in France used natural shapes and imperfections in the rock face as features of their designs.

An artist makes a rapid brushstroke that isn't technically perfect, yet he knows that correcting it doesn't improve his work but rather detracts from its energy. The Japanese enso, the simple circle painted with a single brush stroke, arouses more passion in the beholder than any technically perfect circle. The art is in the movement.

A novelist plans his story, and then at a certain point his fictional characters refuse to fit the mould he has planned for them and begin to take on a life of their own. At this point, the canny novelist gives up rigid control of his plan and goes in the direction the characters are taking. The book then opens up into something more interesting and exciting than the writer could have imagined beforehand.

The skilled hypnotherapist Milton Erickson never confronted his clients, but shifted quickly and invisibly to blend with them, accepting and then utilising their own experience to move without friction towards resolution of their problems. It made every consultation unique.

So many examples: the master of his art balances restriction and freedom, rules and spontaneity. Even a tight deadline gets the juices going. An unsolved problem or impasse pump-primes the process. Necessity truly is the mother of invention.

Maybe the next time you speak with a person you find exasperating, you can tell yourself that this is merely the fault in the block of marble, the creative challenge that is going to spark your ingenuity and creativity in the relationship.

If someone speaks to you about a difficulty they're grappling with, you may think you know how to resolve it and offer a solution. At times this is helpful to the other person; mostly it's not. If, instead, you make no effort to resolve their problem, but enter into it by their side like fish swimming together in the ocean, listening and attending, a solution suddenly pops up *for the other person,* one that suits them better than the solution that would have come from your own reasoning. Conversations, even therapeutic ones, can often be more like improvisation than we think.

AWARENESS ARRIVES WITH THE IN-BREATH

Always, creativity links with breath. Remember a time when a sudden realisation hit you, good or bad – you had a wonderful idea or you realised you had left your wallet behind somewhere. In either case, you experience a sudden intake of breath. Such an in-breath is a moment of spontaneity, to be followed by expression or action. When you react automatically, driven by habit or compulsion, there is no accompanying breath. Response, on the other hand, is your whole mind thinking and feeling and always involves breath. Your breath is the expressive pause that *creates* what follows. It can be infinitesimal or slow and full, but one breath suffices. It is your moment of inspiration, of creativity.

Tennis is a good metaphor for how your creative response works – take, for example, returning the ball. A great player's right-hemisphere holistic scanning is on the case well in advance of any conscious decision-making, at the moment their opponent makes a first almost imperceptible glance or move towards the ball, well before the ball is hit. This moment of awareness is accompanied by an in-breath too.

Breathing out is also valuable: it releases the old – old effort, work, learning, old everything – and paves the way for an involuntary relaxed in-breath that opens the doorway to your subconscious wisdom – your *inspire*-ation.

Intuition: Your Other-than-Conscious Mind

The rational part of our brain that deals with analysis, alternatives, plans and structures in step-by-step progression cannot cope with too many factors at the same time. Creativity is of a different order. There is now sufficient evidence that human intelligence embraces a larger consciousness than the neo-cortex, including not only the right hemisphere of the brain but also body, heart and gut. The more you're able to expand your awareness into all parts of you, the more your subconscious gives you vital information. Your whole mind has access to complexity and subtlety and is capable of producing results that in our uncertainty we like to call serendipity, synchronicity or coincidence.

Yet, as life is busy, many of us use lack of time as an excuse to discount intuition. All the various filters/defaults we discussed earlier also over-ride it. We may understand that grand ideas can emerge from intuition, but have less awareness of how intuition is available to us also on an everyday level – as that quiet little hint of an impulse inside, often a visceral sense rather than a clear thought. It's not at all the same as quick thinking, where a conversationalist finds a smart response from their fund of learned or remembered answers.

Intuition may happen exceedingly often, but most people haven't learned to tune in to its feather touch or are accustomed to ignoring it. Sometimes you know instantly what the signal is telling you; at other times a symbol, an image, a single word, or even a particular story pops into your mind from your subconscious without any as yet definable link to your immediate context. You receive pre-verbal messages as a feeling in the gut, a sinking in the stomach, a shiver of unease, or a taste in the mouth that tells you something is not quite right. All five senses can play a part. Such messages are felt in your body before you have time to formulate language or meaning.

Sometimes you only discover later what it was trying to tell you. But often intuition has an immediate sense of rightness about it. Your brain suddenly registers 'Aha!' and you know you've touched a truth that's come from a deeper source than your intellect. You experience relationships and events suddenly coming together in different patterns, and your chief sensation is one of recognition.

Intuition enables you to sense a truth beyond the stories that another person tells. You feel their pain or confusion and you are curious about everything, but your empathy intuits a truth that doesn't always fit their stories. In a coaching conversation, the intuitive coach pays attention to these messages and learns to trust them. That does not mean that he forces them on the person he is coaching. But he might say, 'This image floated into my mind as you said that. I don't know if it means anything to you?' Or, 'I don't know why, I feel uncomfortable about that. Is that just me, or do you sense something too?' Then he usually lets it go. It may make sense later, or it may not. Such an intervention can often mark the beginning of a particularly useful dialogue. The same applies to conversations with friends or colleagues.

You open the doors of your perception to access something that is wiser than your thinking head. Nothing is worked out; answers pop up and speak to the heart without fixed attitudes, ideas or ideology. You trust your subconscious to work on many different levels and from many different perspectives to understand this current unrepeatable reality here and now in ways that wouldn't be possible with the conscious mind. You use your whole mind by integrating thinking with feeling, and thus make good choices and decisions.

Intuition is sometimes counter-intuitive.

COUNTER-INTUITION

 Keep safe: fly into the face of danger.

The Japanese Tsunami and Counter-Intuition

 All too often, the tiny impulse can feel counter-intuitive – that is, not your habitual way of thinking.

When a catastrophic earthquake hit Japan in 2011, everyone on the island of Oshima rushed to the hills, expecting a tsunami. But experienced fisherman Susumu Sugawara did something different and potentially crazy. He ran to his boat in the harbour and sailed out directly *into* the tsunami. He pushed on full throttle and climbed 20-metre waves, one beyond the next, taller than anything he'd ever seen before, each time scarcely expecting to come through until he saw the horizon again and knew that he had. When the sea finally calmed, and he turned back towards his island, not knowing if it had survived, he had to navigate past wrecked houses and boats floating past. His was the only boat on the island still in one piece, and it proved a lifeline with the mainland in the days and weeks that followed. Sugawara remains a local hero to this day.

In conversation, *saying* the right thing at the right time would often be counter-intuitive if you considered it rationally. Just as the Japanese fisherman faced *into* the wave, sometimes when reason tells you, for instance, to get angry because someone is abusing your relationship, your inner wisdom takes the contrary view and hints at a quieter solution. It can happen the opposite way too: reason or habit warns you to say nothing; the small voice of intuition urges you to speak up.

RECOGNISING INTUITION

You learn to trust your intuition by using it and noticing how it lands. But how do you distinguish your intuition from any old thought that happens to come into your mind? Listening to your intuition is not the same as listening to your own agenda, and only experience allows you to distinguish between the two.

It's not an exact science, certainly, but there are features to look out for:

- Intuition just pops up, fully formed.
- It often seems odd – you find yourself saying or thinking, 'This is a bit weird' or 'Seems crazy, but ...'.
- Sometimes the thing you notice is a synchronicity or a strange coincidence.

In coaching, I sometimes call it the art of blurting – just saying what has come into your mind at that moment. There is wisdom in silence; there's also wisdom at times in loosening your tongue and not worrying about what comes out. Sometimes, such an intervention can be inspired.

How To Develop Intuition

Intuition grows in the healthy environment of a lack of self-consciousness and performance anxiety, acceptance of not knowing, and willingness to make mistakes. You can develop your intuition by getting curious about it in some of these ways:

- Give yourself space – to pay attention, to think, dream and be.
- Capture your thoughts when you awake in the night or on first awakening in the morning by writing them down.
- Catch your first response to people and situations before you form your impression into words. Notice the flutter in your heart, or tension in your stomach, or tightness in your throat, and ask yourself what has prompted those responses.
- Open your mind to serendipities, coincidences, and synchronicities. As spiritual director Henry Morgan suggests, this is like turning a welcome sign on first so that you can become conscious of their presence.

Pretending is a great way to free your mind from habitual responses and open yourself to further possibilities. Pretending is nothing more than acting *as if* something were true.

Acting 'As If'

 Towards the end of my presentation workshops, we sometimes play a game where participants think up scenarios for each other to deliver a part of their presentation 'in the manner of'. For example, one group asked their fellow participant to deliver his presentation in the manner of a wise old man. When he did so, all manner of bad habits fell away; as he adopted the physiology and voice of an old man, his presentation grew in confidence, and he embodied a seriousness and self-belief that was completely absent in his everyday self.

He said afterward that once he felt the surge of confidence that came with being old and wise, all the other pieces fell into place. Most training programmes work to build up competencies one by one. He could have worked at individual competencies for weeks to build up the rooted self-assurance he acquired almost instantly in those few moments of play.

The challenge afterwards was to *believe* what he had just done, and not slip back into 'knowing' that he lacked confidence. If you manage a different way of dealing with a situation through acting 'as if', don't be tempted to discount it later. You did do it; it was you.

LEAVE YOUR EGO OUTSIDE AND 'DISAPPEAR'

Creative conversation comes from *being conscious.* You are not witnessing yourself in action – you are just there *in* the action. It's not the same as taking a dissociated view of the situation like an outside observer. When you acquire presence it's just that, being inside looking out, as opposed to *self*-consciousness, which is an uneasy awareness of people on the outside looking at you.

If I hear a piece of glorious music, I have the beauty of that sound in my consciousness, filling me with joy and awe. But I don't say 'beauty' to myself. If I instantly switch to making conscious meaning, by thinking about how aroused I feel by the sound or by cataloguing the piece or the composer, I've moved to something else. I've put myself at the centre of the experience and it's now about me and what I know. Paradoxically, when you feel as if the universe is revolving around you at its centre, you are living from the ego and are *off*-centre.

Consciousness has no ego. Conversation doesn't exist for us to polish each other's personalities. Your fixed personality, the 'I am ...' – I am an executive coach, a religious counsellor, a caring parent, an effective manager, a powerful leader etc. – disappears. You are left with pure consciousness. Nothing is fixed. You don't consult a particular ideology or set of beliefs. You are alive, responding moment by moment out of your consciousness. When you hear the music, you're caught by it, and you're gone, for in that moment nothing exists but the sound of the music. If you are anywhere, you're inside that sound.

COUNTER-INTUITION

When you are actually at the centre of your universe you disappear.

Clearly, defaults and agendas distort the experience of consciousness. Consciousness is having the mental and physical freedom to be able to respond in the best possible way in a situation. Japanese Zen Buddhist Hakuin Ekaku described it this way: 'If you forget yourself you become the universe. Not lose your *self*, just lose *consciousness* of self so that your intention fuses with the object of attention.' So you *lose* yourself and become completely absorbed in the present moment. That may sound scary, but it is the ideal state for engaging with someone in conversation. Occasionally it just happens. Mostly, it sits the other side of much practice.

Conversation at its best has a glorious spontaneity and flow, where both parties are engaged in a relaxed dialogue, willing to go with the flow, happy with the uncertainty of the moment. In such a moment a phrase may capture a deep truth that will amaze you both; and that is the magic of intuition.

Judith DeLozier's Active Dreaming Practice

Here is a brief description of a creative exercise designed by Judith DeLozier, based on native American 'active dreaming', designed to access your creative wisdom.

- Set your intention to solve whatever problem or question you are posing to yourself.
- Take your time to assume a relaxed state, being happy not to know and with no internal dialogue. Soften your gaze to access your peripheral vision.
- Take a walk in this state, moving with grace and ease, open to whatever happens and ready to notice when the outside world offers you a symbol. Usually, within five or ten minutes something visual or auditory will catch your awareness – or you may step in a puddle!
- Accept whatever is offered. Assume that the symbol is relevant to your original intention.
- *Become* the symbol in your mind, and ask yourself, as the symbol, what characteristics do you have. Are you hard, soft, delicate, rooted, wild? How do these qualities inform your intention?
- Now step into the position of an observer. Notice the relationship between the symbol's information and your intention. What do they make you think of, what connections, what similarities? How does your thinking change with the new information?

6

ENJOY COMMUNION AND THE EMERGENCE OF SOMETHING NEW

> *Human beings are discourse. That flowing moves through you whether you say anything or not. Everything that happens is filled with pleasure and warmth because of the delight of the discourse that's always going on.*
> – Rumi

Awake and aware, vibrating in harmony with another human being, sometimes even in silence, you experience human communion at its most creative. Time slows, barriers dissolve, and both of you lose your sense of a separate self in a phenomenon of generative human communion. Together, you give birth to something new and exciting.

Connect – to Self and Others

What is the real secret of connection between human beings?

Almost everything in this book so far has been about being *available* – open to each other with awareness and energy in the moment. A major part of connection is just that – simply clearing the ground between you, getting rid of social constraints, self-consciousness, control, agendas, criticism and other blocks to openness. But every chapter has also been about *relationship:* attention with open awareness, wholeheartedness, vulnerability, and creative intuition that tunes in to the other person. It is always about presence in front of *a witness,* so that, while you are also present to yourself, you truly see and sense the other person and they truly see and sense you.

SEEING EACH OTHER

This can happen in the simplest of ways. Have you been on a quiet country walk where few people pass and, when they do, you sometimes look at each other and call out some brief greeting? With some people, their faces say nothing at all and the words fall between you. With others, they catch your eye for a second and connect with you; in that brief second you recognise each other: 'Greetings human, I'm human too.'

Various cultures express a sense of communion in the words they use to greet each other. One translation of Sanskrit or Indian *Namaste* is, 'The light in me salutes the light in you.' The African Zulu greeting *Sawubona* says, 'I see you. I see your humanity. I see your dignity and respect.' Seeing and being seen are important parts of our communion with each other. Some writers speak of looking into the soul of another person. When two people gaze into each other's eyes calmly without barriers, something visceral and profound may pass between them. The message is not only 'I am here, and I see you here', but also 'In this moment I am here for you.'

You don't need to be extrovert. You just need to *want* to communicate with real people, and to want to communicate *more* than you want to perform brilliantly or stay in your own bubble or hide. There are many different ways to do it. You can be nervous, excited, calm, peaceful, colourful, tender, strong – any or all of these things. Your way of doing it is fine.

Compare this to what happens when people meet each other with thought agendas. Instead of the eyes focusing, the mind runs its own patter: 'I hope they'll like me. I hope I look okay. I'll make sure I get what I want. I hope I can offload my troubles. I'll make sure this advances my case. I don't feel up for this today.' Such inner noise makes them blind to genuine seeing and alters the look in their eyes for the other person too.

Being seen and validated is hugely important for our wellbeing and development. Psychologist Stephen Gilligan, who has many wise things to say about human relationships, asserts that every human being has to be seen with love and acceptance by other human beings before he can lovingly accept himself, and that every negative experience has to be integrated by the loving human presence of another. In other words, from childhood on, we can't do it on our own. We only fully come into ourselves when we are seen with empathy. As humans, we need sponsoring by other resourceful humans who see and speak to us, touch our spirit, and show us that we matter. This is as true in the workplace as it is at home.

TOUCHING AND HEARING

Touch is another important thread of connection; physical touch of course, but also touch via waves of sound and kinaesthetic sense. When you experience close rapport with someone, you feel *touched* by the connection. Feeling *is* inner touch.

We like to think that we are persuaded by reason, but the bottom line of being convinced is feeling. In the final analysis, something *feels* right, *feels* convincing. Yes, it may feel right because of someone's arguments, but it feels right too because their sound waves *chime in* with our own beliefs, evoke images, memories and emotions; they *resonate* with us on the same *wavelength;* we feel *in tune.*

The words we use to describe these feelings are associated with both sound and hearing. Sound plays a bigger part in communication than people have realised up till now. When someone speaks, their sound waves travel through the air and, reaching you, they oscillate inside and you feel the quality of that vibration. When words are violent, you experience the violence in your body. You say, 'He *bombarded* me with questions. I feel *battered.* She *lay into* me.' Compare that with the experience of someone speaking from the heart. The caring quality in the voice touches and soothes you.

Your voice is a wonderfully subtle instrument. Beyond liking and not liking someone's voice, there are subtleties of vibration that communicate with us beyond consciousness. Every word you utter resonates slightly differently according to the energy you give to it and affects your listener in different ways. For example, a subtle lightness of tone in a word or phrase may lighten the spirit of the other person, perhaps even without them realising what has happened. The natural gentle vibration of your voice low in your chest when you describe something you love may convey to the other person that you're wholehearted about it, without the necessity of words to explain. I've described this phenomenon elsewhere.

A Man to do Business With

 What was it that led UK Prime Minister Margaret Thatcher to announce, 'I like Mr Gorbachev: we can do business together', after meeting the President of the Soviet Union? Mikhail Gorbachev himself suspected it was his ability to make her laugh. His interpreter in a report back in Moscow, afterwards, mentioned Gorbachev's charm and self-assurance as well as his 'naturalness' as he calmly searched for the right phrase before giving voice. His voice was described as lively and strong, a huge contrast to the traditionally stony voices of the Soviet leadership. What is clear is that his whole demeanour, voice, and nonverbal language contained a spark that connected, beyond opinions and beliefs. Indeed, Margaret Thatcher mentioned afterwards that it was easy to discuss differences with him.

There are specific tools you can use to encourage connection in conversation. The easiest way to get on the same wavelength is by adjusting your voice, language, and physiology to match the other person. This simply means that if the other person speaks softly, you speak a bit softer too; if they move and gesture as they speak, you show more movement too; if they are energetic, you increase your energy too; and they register the similarity instinctively and feel more in tune with you. You find that you do much of this naturally when you get on well with someone.

But, when you adjust to another person deliberately, even if you intend your adjustment as a graceful acknowledgment of their way of being rather than a manipulation to get them to like you or do your bidding, it is still a doing; and connection is more about *being* than doing. Even without adopting specific techniques, when you are open and available to the other person your breathing automatically synchronises with theirs and you become attuned to their way of being. You *entrain* to each other; your vibrations – your energy or Ki – resonate together. In scientific parlance, your mirror neurons fire. This is how you feel 'felt' by another person. As humans, we find the experience healing and freeing.

Resonating with the other person doesn't mean that you lose awareness of differences between you. Indeed, the right hemisphere of your brain delights in the freshness of difference. But you are in the presence of a harmonising energy, a unifying force. Rumi would say that the lamps are different, but the light is one. It's much more than an interest in each other or an interest in a mutual topic of conversation. You get in tune with each other's vibrations, their internal state comes into your awareness, and you sing in harmony. When that happens, the whole created by the two of you is larger than the sum of your individual parts.

Love Energy

In some interesting research on relationships at the University of California, Davis Emilio Ferrer found that couples in a romantic relationship breathed at the same rate as each other and their hearts beat at the same rate too – they were indeed in harmony. This effect was not evident with people who were not couples.

Daniel Siegel notes in *The Mindful Therapist* that when people are in harmony with each other, not only do heart rates and breathing align, but even shifts in EEG findings and heart rate variability match.

The physicist and psychotherapist Barbara Brennan observes in her book *Hands of Light* that healers can detect how different emotions vibrate at different frequencies in the body. The feeling of love generates more energy – a faster vibration and higher frequency – than the feeling of fear.

A critical attitude produces something rather different. When you judge, you want to get rid of something in the other person, and you go on the attack – if only in your own head. Judgement, even when unspoken, is always registered on some level as an attack. It's only when we accept each other that we draw close and find there was nothing to reject at all, for as soon as the whole person is accepted, then anything negative dissolves in the light of day – not got rid of, but integrated.

You can't leave yourself out of it. If you approach others with lots of questions but hide and protect your own core self, they have no possibility of communion with *you*, however much sympathy they receive *from* you, simply because there is no tangible you for them to connect with. They may even feel exposed, after revealing personal information to you, if they fail to receive openness in return. If you are a coach or in a therapeutic role, you will certainly have learned that it's inappropriate to bring your own 'stuff' into the conversation to muddy the waters. But that doesn't mean you leave yourself out of the relationship. You need to be fully and empathically present, not hiding behind your role.

True Empathy

Empathy is feeling. When I empathise with your pain, I don't feel empathy, I feel pain. Various different emotions get passed off as empathy. 'Isn't it awful?' someone exclaims. 'They lost absolutely everything. It's really sad.' And even as they speak you hear pleasure mixed in with the drama – pleasure at being the one to report the news; schadenfreudian pleasure at knowing it's not them. They don't suffer pain. You might call that sympathy or pity, but it's not empathy.

True empathy means to feel the full strength of another's feeling without drowning inside it. It's to be in the deep ocean with the other person and, by maintaining your own integrity, to prevent them from drowning too. There is an important difference between my feeling sad because you look sad, as mirror neurons fire in my body, and feeling empathy while my deep consciousness is able to distinguish between your sadness and mine. Without this awareness, I am likely to be overwhelmed by your negative emotion and get lost in your sadness, as your pain locks onto my own. This happens particularly with emotions that I've yet to process within myself, including anger and frustration. In order to navigate safely through this danger of being overwhelmed, I have to have a healthy relationship with myself that includes a firm sense of me. I mean 'me' as in my deep consciousness, not 'me' as in my ego.

COUNTER-INTUITION

You merge with the other person AND you are still whole and separate.

KNOW THYSELF

Conversation works when you cross the bridge to another person without losing yourself in the process. You can't properly cross the bridge to another without first crossing the bridge to yourself. All relationship is a reflection of your relationship with yourself. Other people can't draw close to you until you have a close, compassionate relationship with yourself.

This is not the same at all as being aware of your impact, or worse, being self-consciously and painfully aware of what you are feeling. With self-consciousness your looking is a loop that sees only yourself as you imagine yourself from the other person's eyes. The tension this creates makes you forfeit spontaneity and become stiff and lifeless or heavy with effort. Self-consciousness is usually full of self-criticism as well, and if your relationship with yourself is judgemental you take judgement into your relationships with others.

What conversations do you have with yourself? Some people are remarkably unkind. They run themselves down, label themselves stupid, even slap themselves physically when they make a mistake. Turn that behaviour outward and you'd want to run a mile.

Self-Compassion Practice

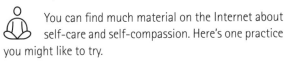 You can find much material on the Internet about self-care and self-compassion. Here's one practice you might like to try.

- Think of any scenario where you feel loving kindness; it might be towards a child or an animal or indeed anything on this planet or beyond.

- Take time to feel that kindness within yourself. How does it express itself? In touch, affirming words, a feeling of warmth?
- Now turn that loving kindness in whatever way it expresses itself inwards to yourself.
- If you get that feeling when you stroke a cat, then stroke yourself, one arm stroking another, stroking your shoulders, your cheeks, your face.
- If it expresses itself in words, speak kind words to yourself, either out loud or inside your head. The words don't always have to be such expressions as, 'You are wonderful'. Sometimes, something as simple as 'You're okay: you're really okay' is enough.
- If it expresses itself in feeling, as it certainly will, then enjoy feelings of warmth or softness inside yourself.

The practice takes just a minute or two. At the end, thank yourself for the loving attention.

Empathy requires you to be fully present. In risking showing the other person your human spirit, you find true expression and have no further need of social props and techniques. Empathy is powerful. It is your greatest gift to the other person as well as to yourself.

The Best Help Ever

 M. Scott Peck tells a surprising story in *The Road Less Travelled* of the best help he ever had. As a young man, unable to make a decision about whether to leave school or continue studying, he asked three responsible adults he knew for advice. The first two, his personal adviser and the dean of his school, advised him to continue with his studies. The last person he asked, his brilliant maths teacher, listened to him for much longer than the other two, and then finally said he felt that if he were in Scott Peck's shoes he wouldn't know what to do either, so he couldn't help him.

Scott Peck was close to desperation at the time and thinks that this last answer saved his life. For, he reasoned, if a genius found the decision hard, there was no shame in *his* finding it hard. If a genius didn't tell him his idea of dropping out was mad, maybe it wasn't mad after all. So he left school. The maths teacher succeeded in crossing the bridge where others had failed and without offering a single word of advice gave the boy what he needed – a way to trust himself. The teacher's gift was in bringing the whole of himself into their relationship.

Each of us knows at certain times what it is to be in a happy relationship with ourselves. Those moments are revealed in your answers to such questions as, 'When have you felt most fully yourself?' or 'When have you been so immersed in something that time and even you disappear?' It might be when you are listening to music, or when you are stargazing, or painting, running, reading, walking in nature, or talking with someone close to you. In such moments you have a felt sense of the experience; you are energised by it and find it easy to use the word love: I love dancing, I love walking in the countryside, I love stargazing. At these times you find the freedom to be your spontaneous self. You live in your own centre, not at some distance from yourself. Inward human and outward human are one.

Now, imagine taking such *immersion* into your conversation with someone. In this loving space, spontaneity is able to emerge with its magic.

Being in the Space

When you are self-compassionate, you are able to trust yourself, and this enhances your trust in the other person. You see yourself as a part of a whole and become curious about your differences. The conversation becomes a co-creation.

In the martial art of Aikido, a student learns how to follow the energy of her attacker to begin to exert influence and lead to a good outcome. To follow in this art requires mental alertness and somatic awareness to work together. Then at a certain point the advanced student becomes aware that there is no more following – she is pure awareness in the space moving towards harmony. She has transformed from a *doing* into a *being*.

Merging with Your Art

 You might have an experience of *being* in any art or science in which you gain high skill. In *Zen in the Art of Archery*, Eugen Herrigel writes about the moment after years of practice that an archer becomes empty of self and at one with his arrow. At that point he attains his highest art, as skill breaks through to a quite different and joyful experience of being not doing. A master musician may experience something similar. She never *masters* her instrument but joins with it. The resulting music is neither musician nor instrument yet comes about because of both.

And so it happens that one day you are talking with someone, and you reach a point where no one is leading: you both *are*, in a place of in-between, both swimming in a beautiful sea of co-existence. You feel a powerful frisson of connection within that space. Eckhart Tolle calls it a 'field of awareness' and suggests that it becomes the primary purpose of your interactions.

The characters for *human being* in Japanese mean *person* and *between,* suggesting that as human beings we exist only through our relations with others. People in the Western world, with its emphasis on personal success, might find the idea surprising. The field of awareness between you is the space where creativity happens, where there is no you, no me, but just the space you create together. In this space, 'you' and 'me' no longer have fixed qualities as in the controlled ego. There's no image to sustain and no fear of consequence. You are free to find in yourself whatever is needed here and now, be it strength or gentleness, power or playfulness. It's an exhilarating experience.

Communication is More than Words

Conversation is, of course, talking to each other. When you meet someone, what do you think about if not what to say? Most people get very good at making conversation and slip easily into a 'public' mode of small talk and other exchanges suitable for particular occasions, but it's simplistic to describe conversation as straightforward talking. For a start, people often don't say what they mean; in fact, quite often through embarrassment or fear they can lead you *away* from what they really mean. There's much going on under the surface.

What people *don't* say when they talk to each other is as impor-tant, and probably more so, than what they do say. A response such as 'I don't know', delivered in a flat voice, is as likely to mean, 'I don't care, I'm angry and you don't understand me' as to be a simple assertion of lack of knowledge. This is why the right-brain's ability to pick up tone, inflection, metaphor and symbol, humour and paradox, is so important. When someone with left-brain confidence quotes someone's words as proof of something, they are leaving out the bigger part of meaning. The media, politicians, and business grandees do this all the time: 'I believe that in 1962 *you said* …'. It's important to realise that while actual words are mainly the province of the left-brain, most other elements of communication – including meaning, inference, intention, context, tone, facial expression, gesture, humour, irony and metaphor – are the province of the right-brain. What you *are* always speaks louder than what you say. The novelist Peter Carey suggested that the declared meaning of a spoken sentence is only its overcoat, and that the real meaning lies underneath its scarves and buttons. The quality of your thoughts and feelings has an impact on the other person, whatever words you use.

Sometimes, the apparent subject of a conversation is not even the real subject of the conversation, and both parties in some bit of themselves know it. You might have an end of life con-versation with someone, and you talk about whether the pillow is comfortable, and whether sleep is hard to achieve, yet the whole conversation is a way of saying, 'I love you', and the other person, without remarking on the fact, hears this simply and directly. If you were a fly on the wall to this conversation, you would read the real meaning in the tone of voice, the look in the eyes, and many other tiny cues. Sometimes, language is symbolic, and what needs to be said can find expression only in images.

STILLNESS AND SILENCE

Besides, much happens between words. As in music, the silences between sounds are as significant as the sounds themselves. In conversation, silences are full of meaning. Good coaches, teachers, and counsellors know that they can be *too* good at asking questions and keeping the flow of conversation going. Leaving a silence allows the other person space and sometimes produces a revelation.

I once listened to someone tell me about her problem for 10 or 15 minutes. At the end of that time, she thanked me warmly. 'I now know exactly what to do', she said. I hadn't said a single word. But I had been listening. I'm not saying that my listening solved her problem, but it was the *catalyst* that helped her unconscious to solve her problem. It is said that the sculptor Michelangelo could already see the finished form of his work in a block of stone, and his job was to release it. As catalyst, you allow the other person to release an answer that is already there for them to find.

When you listen to information and not the silence, you miss the quality of being in the space. You think that things need to happen, that you need to do something, when in the silence what you need is already present.

Rumi wrote in one of his Discourses: 'Speech is always within you whether you actually speak or not, even if you have no thought of speaking.' We influence each other by what we don't say. Inside my head I can be angry about a relationship – completely! – or I can be happy and loving and grateful for it; my perception changes everything. Most of us think that such thoughts remain in our heads, but because we are always communicating, our silence communicates as loudly as our words. Some part of the other person's consciousness has an inkling of what is going on inside our head.

When you allow silence, you expand possibilities. At first it can feel awkward. As soon as there is a pause in conversation you may be tempted to rush into words to fill the gap. But if you can just *be* with the silence, this is where communion starts. Allow the pause and wait for words to come if they want to. When you become comfortable with silence, idle chatter seems empty and futile. People who have been on a silent retreat often remark upon return to normal life that much conversation now feels pointless or superfluous.

Quietness in Song

 When I was studying opera, I read *How to Sing* by Lillie Lehmann, a nineteenth-century opera star. She said that the first thing required for a singer at the beginning of a performance was to remain quiet: 'The quieter the singer or artist, the more significant is every expression he gives; the fewer motions he makes, the more importance they have. So he can scarcely be quiet enough.' But, she continued, this quietness is the opposite of indifference, as it is achievable only because the artist is fully in command of herself, and this power is a reassurance to the audience. Her description might well apply to the silence of a listener in conversation, too.

Silence, like stillness, is full of movement. Even when still and quiet, you are always breathing. I think of a tower that naturally sways slightly at the top; were you to force it to be still the rigidity would be injurious to the structure. So too with silence: when the

Buddha is sitting in still and silent meditation, there is a dance of consciousness within. The still point is nothing but the centre of a dance or the eye of a storm. A propeller spins at great speed and appears still: all movement, yet all stillness.

Movement Within Stillness

 Gaze for a few moments at this circular image and witness its movement. It is of course a still image, even as it appears to move and vibrate. Feel the stillness and energetic movement at the same time.

If we usually understand *communication* as the words we speak to each other, *communion* is the energetic connection, heart to heart, that has no need of words – alive but still. The Chinese philosopher Chuang-Tzu said that the whole universe surrenders to a mind that is still.

COUNTER-INTUITION

Silence speaks loudly.

In silence and stillness, your body expresses more than words ever can – deep truths that have no language. You might think that a silent listener contributes little, but silent attention is *all* that is needed. W. B. Yeats wrote in *The Celtic Twilight* that 'we can make our minds so like still water that beings gather about us that they may see, it may be, their own images, and so live for a moment with a clearer, perhaps even with a fiercer life because of our quiet'.

CREATIVITY IN THE SPACE

Beautiful experiences in conversation are seldom pre-planned and it's hard to measure their usefulness at the time. They happen in those in-between moments and what emerges might surprise everyone.

The necessity of specific intended results in order to attract funding is the catch-22 of scientific research today. If you get funding only to find the answer to a particular stated problem, your quest is self-enclosed and self-referring; you never go off piste into the field of possibilities where amazing new discoveries can be made. We've already seen how the history of invention is full of happy accidents and serendipities that take steps into the unknown. When two people meet, you can aim for 2 + 2 = 4, and if you stick to procedure that is probably what you will get. But in the creative space of relationship and possibility the answer could well be $2 + 2 = 5$ or 20 or 100 – far beyond the sum of its parts.

A Special Russian Meeting – Gorbachev again

 At a difficult point of the Cold War, Aleksandr Yakovlev, the Soviet Ambassador to Canada, met Mikhail Gorbachev, then an active member of the Politburo, on the occasion of a dinner party for Soviet Union dignitaries. They didn't know each other. It just happened that their Canadian host's arrival was severely delayed, and they were thrown together for several hours while waiting for him to arrive. The two decided to take a stroll to pass the time and ended up walking and talking for three hours. Gradually, they abandoned caution and became more frank and open with each other, eventually trusting each other enough to bring up such dangerous topics as perestroika and glasnost. When Gorbachev became head of the Soviet Union a couple of years later, he appointed Yakovlev to be one of his chief advisers in implementing perestroika and glasnost.

Without a specific purpose in their meeting, they were less interested in the usefulness of the other person than in mutual understanding. That created the climate for connection and trust. Later, when Gorbachev needed an adviser, he thought of a man he had learned to trust.

When your heart expands in the space to encompass both of you, anything is possible. Edwin Markham describes it beautifully in his little epigram, *Outwitted*:

> *He drew a circle that shut me out –*
> *Heretic, rebel, a thing to flout.*
> *But love and I had the wit to win:*
> *We drew a circle and took him in!*

This larger creative conversational space is the province of the right hemisphere of the brain. While the left hemisphere concentrates on the content of a conversation, putting forward arguments and intending a direction towards an outcome, the right hemisphere attends to the space between you in this moment and your presence in relationship to each other. In the absence of specific rules of engagement, you are faced with this moment, this place, these aspects of you and me, now, here, today. This space is the world of both/and, paradox, metaphor, and humour, where uncertainty goes hand in hand with limitless possibility, and truth though present is too complex to be fully expressed in words. You both operate from a deeper more trusting place.

You may like to come back to breathing for a few moments to experience the gentle holding of this generative space. It's good to practise, so that you can use this breath at certain important moments to find your calm when you are in communication with someone. Often, a single breath is enough.

Enter into the Moment of Connection

- Breathe slowly in through your nose with awareness that this is your breath of entry into the present moment. Imagine it is not you breathing but the universe breathing *you*.

- Experience your body relaxing and expanding in every direction into infinity as it fills with air, giving you a sense of calm.
- As the air fills you, feel its wise energy enter the space between your eyes.
- Enjoy the moment of space as you breathe slowly out through your nose.
- Repeat a few times.

It's All Love

The English word 'love' sags under the weight of all the meaning thrust upon it. Other languages have a variety of words for different kinds of love; in English we are stuck with the one word. It is particularly difficult to interpret when treated as a noun, as in, 'What is love?' or 'I'm looking for love'. It definitely sounds like something outside of us. And are we talking about sexual love, companionship, friendship, love for a child, a neighbour, love of humanity, or love of life?

We know more about the word as a verb – to love. When you love someone, you feel a sensation that comes in many forms yet is unmistakeable. Loving is active: it has energy. When we love, we feel its power, and we love not only the object of our intimacy, but nothing less than everything. The whole world seems a brighter, lighter space, and we feel in closer communion with people and nature. The universe feels harmonious; fighting, anger, and war seem stupid and unnecessary. The energy of love is evident throughout the world in the care that humans and animals show for each other. We might find it easier to call it *loving kindness*.

When you encounter loving or caring in conversation, you feel attended to. You are met exactly where you are with empathy and understanding. You connect with an energy you trust that makes you feel safe. These elements of love apply to all conversations, with friend, client, competitor, family, or stranger. Love captures the whole at a glance and spontaneously says or does something that has a sense of rightness about it, in ways that sometimes seem miraculous. Loving has its own wisdom. It sees the most beautiful part of you and allows you to see it too. It even sees parts of you that are yet to emerge and awakens the beauty in you.

If you are most concerned about communication in a business context, this might seem too soft. But think about someone at work who cares about how you are and what happens to you, and the difference that makes. Love is not all red roses and sentiment; it exists, too, in the occasional glance of understanding, and in someone's appreciation of what you have to offer.

Last Day of School

 At my secondary school, two of us applied to Oxford University. My friend was awarded a place; I was not. At 18 years of age, it was a longstanding dream shattered, the biggest disappointment of my life. On the last day of school, I was in a small group saying goodbye to staff, and I heard one teacher congratulate my friend on getting into Oxford. A few moments later another elderly teacher, Miss Avis, said to me quietly, 'Remember Judy, you can do *anything*'. I'm not sure I really understood her meaning. But, catching me at that low point, and perhaps awakening something in me that I was unable to see at that time, her words remained with me. Many a time since, when life has seemed tough, I've been able to say to myself, 'I can do *anything*', and feel renewed courage and optimism. Her encouragement has lasted a lifetime.

When someone is responsive to need at moments in our life, we don't always understand at the time to what extent we have internalised the feeling of being cared for. But the memory of a feeling in relationship to another person lives on in us, giving us recurring pleasure and resilience for later challenges. If we are to give that support to others, we have to be awake and aware. The right words at the right time can indeed last a lifetime. What an awesome opportunity for teachers, managers, leaders, and all of us.

Beyond Words in Football

 While studying NLP in Santa Cruz, I heard the story of a well-known but rather gruff football manager, who was interviewed about the success of his team. The reporter asked, 'Tell our viewers, what *is* the secret of your success?' He expected the manager's views on fitness and resilience, team selection, training or game strategy. Better known for his skill on the field than for his power with words, the manager struggled to express himself. The interviewer tried again. There was a long silence. Then the manager suddenly burst out, 'Goddammit, I just love the b***ards!'

LOVE IN BUSINESS? YOU MUST BE JOKING

It is very easy to dismiss love. It's all too intangible and is allotted little serious place in our highly organised, technologically advanced world. Many company executives would suggest that it's too indulgent and not relevant in the work sphere. It's quite common for business people to have one way of communicating at work and a different way with their family. If asked to describe the differences in a few words, one person might use *authoritative, decisive,* and *hard-headed* for work, and *loving, generous,* and *laid-back* for home.

Working with executives in corporations, I have frequently come across examples of these differences. I coached a senior manager who on careful nudging told me about happy holidays with his partner but thought it 'unprofessional' to find out anything about his staff beyond their competence to do their current job.

On another occasion, I spotted an old boss chatting to friends in a pub. At work she didn't want staff to talk to her beyond the briefest work headlines.

There's a growing assumption that work life has completely different rules, not only from home life, but from life itself full-stop. There was the company owner who sacked a member of staff for one mistake. 'We don't make mistakes in this company', he asserted. Really? Then there was the partner in a law firm who, at the end of four coaching sessions, asked me hesitantly if the interpersonal skills he was finding useful might possibly help him to create friendships outside work. I assured him they could.

We can see today how 'hard-headed' approaches divide the world ever more into factions opposed to each other, and the rhetoric becomes ever more aggressive and bullying. But realise this: if I have no connection with you and I attack you, your response is going to be self-defence and counter-attack – no question. But if I succeed in making connection with you, even slightly, then I can bring up disagreement without bullying and, in so doing, I give the process a chance of moving forward. Parents' admonitions said with love hit home. Bullying creates bullies. We all recognise the power of this in the private sphere. If given a chance, it works in the public sphere too.

The most successful leaders use both left-brain *and* right-brain skills, both/and. They are both authoritative, decisive, and hard-headed *and* loving, generous, *and* laid-back. It's about playing the whole keyboard, using all your resources, not just those traditionally associated with business. It's sometimes more important to show a member of staff that you care about them than to show them that you are authoritative. It's sometimes more important to give a colleague leeway than to insist on something done your way. In the end, leadership is more about the choices you make in the moment than the rules you subscribe to.

Playing the Whole Keyboard

You might like to experiment with introducing qualities from one part of your life into another.

- For example, if listening to your partner is something you do without hurry or impatience at home, try out that way of being with one of your reports or a colleague at work. See what emerges when you give them time to say what they need to say.
- If you are decisive at work, experiment with being more definite about your ideas and wants at home and see how your family reacts.
- If you are easy-going at home, see what happens if you bring this quality into a work meeting and let things happen for a while, releasing your usual tight control over the agenda.

If you carry out these experiments without prejudice, you may realise that some of the changes work well for you and give you increased options and better results.

Creating Change

I was almost at the end of this book when I came across the work of Otto Scharmer at MIT. He describes four different fields of conversation, which resonate with what I've been describing.

1. The first field he calls habitual, or 'talking nice', and it has much in common with the kind of social conversation I describe in the chapter on control.

2. The second field is conversational debate, similar to some of the competitive agendas I describe, where each person holds to his or her fixed opinion and spars with his conversational opponent. The positions are set out at the start, and the differences between the two sides remain at the end. This kind of conversation rarely leads to a genuine resolution, only a temporary winner and loser.

3. The third field is dialogue, where both parties engage in openhearted enquiry and there is more scope for flexibility. Here, the two conversationalists explore each other's ideas and there may even be some movement towards each other.

4. The fourth field goes one step further. Each person becomes an open presence to the other, and they co-generate their conversation in a state of flow. The fluidity is such that out of difference something entirely new is generated. Ideas arise from their joining, and they might be hard-pressed to know exactly who had come up with any particular new thought.

COUNTER-INTUITION

 You're essential and you don't matter at all.

In such conversations there's an understanding that two opposite ideas can both be true at the same time. A situation can be both tragic and comic. It's possible to understand very well and understand absolutely nothing in the same breath. As you hold the tension of opposites wholeheartedly without slipping into opposition, there comes an expansion of what you know and feel and something new and more universal is given the opportunity to emerge.

This suggests that we are changed not so much by others' beliefs and opinions as by our experience of close connection, which opens heart and mind to something new. There has been much discussion recently of how young men and sometimes women are radicalised and turn to terrorism. It turns out that before new and extreme ideas take root, these young people very often encounter qualities of acceptance and closeness with their new group that were absent in their life before. First the connection, and the ideas follow. Dan Siegel, a pioneer in the emerging field of Interpersonal Neurobiology, explains that we are shaped by our *experiences* in interpersonal relationships; our brains are changed by the focus of our attention in our communication with each other. This would suggest that, though society's left-brain instinct might be to fix a problem with some form of correction, *wholehearted connection* is one of the most important gifts we can offer to young people.

Last Words on the Planet

Communication is never just a message: it's a sharing of meaning. George Bernard Shaw famously quipped that: 'The single biggest problem in communication is the illusion that it has taken place.' The one thing that often *doesn't* happen when one person talks to others is the sharing of meaning, however many words they speak. The message received simply fails to resemble the message spoken.

The left-brain likes to divide and categorise in every sphere of life. It may be that you speak about a serviette, whereas I talk about a napkin. I then take that difference as the symbol of other differences. You have a Lancashire accent, while I speak in what I like to call 'received pronunciation'; you say 'Hi' and I say 'Good morning', and on and on and on. So, I make generalisations about who you are from bits of information and create a belief system based upon it.

Sharing of meaning arises from the attention of our right-brain. I notice your individuality, that you are a particularly gentle kind of man, that you like living things, that you show courage when you notice something unjust. In seeing what is individual and real about you, I sense and feel our connection in the human condition. From the individual I find the universal.

When we join the essence of who we are with the essence of who you are, then meaning is deeper, more resonant. Whatever our respective roles, we join in simple human connection. The trust that makes this possible is the essential element of communion. It's a joining where we are both self-aware and other-aware.

It's interesting with what frequency the most brilliant scientists appreciate the wonder of communion. Albert Einstein put it powerfully in a note of comfort to a man whose son had died:

A human being is part of the whole world, called by us 'Universe,' a part limited in time and space. He experiences himself, his thoughts and feelings as something separate from the rest – a kind of optical delusion of his consciousness. The striving to free oneself from this delusion is the one issue of true religion. Not to nourish the delusion but to try to overcome it is the way to reach the attainable measure of peace of mind.

We need our left hemisphere for its energy and practicality, but not on its own. The pre-eminence of our right-brain over the left is absolutely essential if we are to humanise the grandiosity of our pattern-making abstract-thinking left-brain – and save our planet in the process.

Think of any of the dilemmas of our age – pollution, climate change, excessive nationalism, racism, conflict between nations ... We can be clever and individualistic; we can get ahead, have the last word, be certain and win battles. Or we can take the interconnected route and find meaningful ways to engage that give the planet a chance. This means finding ways to meet each other, not forever categorising, dividing and sub-dividing: continent from continent, country from country, capitalism from socialism, white skin from dark skin, urban from rural, gated community from council estate, privately educated from publicly educated, young from old. The long future, for ourselves, our families, communities, businesses, and the planet itself depends on connectivity across the globe, including our moment to moment connections, here in the palm of our hands.

The way we interact with the world, and therefore the way we communicate, changes our *brains*. If we want a future, our kind, uncertain, humour-loving, holistic right-brain is the most powerful weapon we possess.

PEOPLE INDEX

Arrau, Claudio: 1903–1991, Chilean pianist.

Barks, Coleman: American poet who has written numerous poetic interpretations of the works of Rumi. Books include *A Year with Rumi*, *Rumi: The Big Red Book*, and *Rumi: Selected Poems*.

Beckes, Lane and Coan, James A.: Psychologists, University of Virginia USA. Their article 'Social baseline theory: the role of social proximity in emotion and economy of action' was published in *Social and Personality Psychology Compass*. http://www.cfhmc.com/wp-content/uploads/2016/06/SocialBaselineTheory.pdf.

Beethoven, Ludwig Van: 1770–1827, German composer. Information about his creative process from a letter to Louis Schlosser 1822/1823. Comment about his improvisation from *Beethoven, the Man and the Artist: As Revealed in His Own Words* (1905) edited by Friedrich Kerst.

Blake, William: 1757–1827, English poet and artist. Quotation from *The Marriage of Heaven and Hell*.

Bowden, E. M. and Jung-Beeman, M.: Psychologists at Northwestern University USA. Their 2003 article, 'Aha! Insight experience correlates with solution activation in the right hemisphere', appeared in the *Psychonomic Bulletin & Review*, 10, 730–737. https://cpb-us-e1.wpmucdn.com/sites.northwestern.edu/dist/a/699/files/2015/11/Aha-Insight-experience-correlates-with-solution-activation-in-the-right-hemisphere-2n5zk69.pdf.

Brennan, Barbara: American physicist and spiritual healer. Observation from her book, *Hearts of Light*.

Brown, Brene: American research professor, author and speaker. Ted Talk on vulnerability, *ted.com/talks/brene_brown_on_vulnerability.html* plus various books including *Daring Greatly*.

Carey, Mariah: American singer and songwriter. Wrote tribute to Stevie Wonder, steviewonder.org.uk.

Carey, Peter: Australian novelist. Quoted in Colum McCann's article, the *Guardian Review* 13 May 2017.

Casals, Pablo: 1876–1973, Catalan cellist. See *Casals and the Art of Interpretation* by David Blum, p. 161.

Chopin, Kate: 1850–1904, American author. Quotation from her novel, *Awakening*, p. 216.

Chuang-Tzu: Fourth century BCE, Chinese philosopher, traditional author of the *Chuang-Tzu*.

Churchill, Sir Winston: 1874–1965, British prime minister twice between 1940 and 1955. Remarks by F. E. Smith from Speaker's Lecture delivered by Sir Nicholas Soames MP, 2011.

Cohen, Leonard: 1934–2016, Canadian singer-songwriter, poet and novelist. Remarks from his speech at the 2011 Prince of Asturias Awards. https://www.youtube.com/watch?v=VIR5ps8usuo.

cummings, e e: 1894–1962, American poet. Poem, 'I thank you god' from *e e cummings: Selected Poems*.

Degas, Edgar: 1834–1917, painter and sculptor; quoted in *Artists on Art: From the XIV to the XX Century*, ed. Robert Goldwater.

DeLozier, Judith: American author, trainer and co-developer of NLP. Active Dreaming exercise adapted from her article, 'Mastery, new coding and systemic NLP', published in *NLP World*, 2:1, March 1995.

Dench, Judi: English actress. Quotes taken from interview with Tim Adams in the *Observer*. https://www.theguardian.com/film/2012/oct/14/judi-dench-interview-skyfall.

Desplat, Dr Juliette: Head of Modern Overseas, Intelligence & Security Records at the National Archives. Meeting of Margaret Thatcher and Mikhail Gorbachev discussed in her book *A Man One Could Do Business With*. https://blog.nationalarchives.gov.uk/blog/man-one-business/.

Einstein, Albert: 1879–1955, German-born theoretical physicist. Words from a letter to a father who has lost his young son. Quote on the intellect from Einstein's *Out of My Later Years*, p. 260.

Ferrer, Emilio: Researcher at University of California Davis USA. See article by Karen Nikos-Rose on his research on lovers' hearts beating in sync in *Science & Technology*, 8 February 2013. https://www.ucdavis.edu/news/lovers-hearts-beat-sync-uc-davis-study-says/.

Feynman, Richard: 1918–1988, American theoretical physicist. Words from interview for BBC *Horizon* Programme, *The Pleasure of Finding Things Out*, 1981.

Foy, Claire: English actress. Interview with Tom Lamont, the *Guardian* 29 September 2018. https://www.theguardian.com/culture/2018/sep/29/claire-foy-my-anxiety-was-a-tool-to-survive.

Fun Theory, The: The Piano Staircase Initiative was one of a series of experiments in DDB Worldwide Communications Group Inc.'s new brand campaign for Vollkswagen. See video: https://www.youtube.com/watch?v=SByymar3bds™t=3s.

Gallwey, Tim: American author of series of *Inner Game* books. Comments from his presentation at the ICF Conference 1999.

Gelb, Michael J.: American author of *How to Think Like Leonardo Da Vinci*.

Gilligan, Stephen: American psychologist. Comments from his book *The Courage to Love*.

Gladwell, Malcolm: Canadian journalist and author. Korean pilot story from his book, *Outliers*.

Gorbachev, Mikhail: Head of State of USSR 1988–1991. Meeting with Thatcher described in the National Archives: https://blog.nationalarchives.gov.uk/blog/man-one-business/. Story of meeting with Aleksandr Yakovlev from *The Soviet Ambassador: The Making of the Radical Behind Perestroika* by Christopher Shulgan.

Graham, Martha: American modern dancer and choreographer. Quotation from *The Life and Work Of Martha Graham - A Biography*, by Agnes De Mille, 1991.

Hakuin Ekaku: 1686–1768, Influential figure in Japanese Zen Buddhism.

Herrigel, Eugen: 1884–1955, German philosopher and author of *Zen in the Art of Archery.*

Hopkins, Gerard Manley: 1844–1889, English poet and Jesuit priest. Lines from his poem about a kestrel, *The Windhover.*

Johnson, Wilko: English singer, guitarist and songwriter. Kyoto story recounted in his *Guardian* article, 10 June 2015. https://www.theguardian.com/travel/2015/jun/10/dr-feelgood-wilko-johnson-shunkoin-temple-kyoto-japan.

Jung, Carl: 1875–1961, Swiss psychiatrist and psychoanalyst. Quotation from David Sedgwick's *Introduction to Jungian Psychotherapy: The Therapeutic Relationship*, p. 8.

Kafka, Franz: 1883–1924, Austrian (Czechoslovakian-born) writer. Quotation from his *Parables and Paradoxes*, 1946.

Keats, John: 1795–1821, English Romantic poet. Quotation from a letter to George and Thomas Keats, 22 December 1817.

Kennedy, Nigel: English violinist. Comments from his autobiography *Always Playing.*

Kingsolver, Barbara: American author. Quote from *Animal Dreams*, p. 220.

Lehmann, Lilli: 1848–1929, German operatic soprano. Lines from her book, *How to Sing*, 1902.

Linklater, Kristin: Scottish vocal coach and acting teacher. Quotation from her book, *Freeing the Natural Voice*, p 51.

Malone, Gareth: English choirmaster and broadcaster, presenter of the BBC2 show, *The Choir*. His words recorded by Jackee Holder in her Vulnerability Project: https://thevulnerabilityproject.wordpress .com/2014/01/11/jackee-holder/comment-page-1/.

Markham, Edwin: 1852–1940, American poet. *Outwitted* is one of a number of epigrams he wrote.

Matisse, Henri: 1869–1954, French artist. *Jazz* was a limited-edition art book of his paper collages accompanied by his handwritten thoughts, issued in 1947.

McGilchrist, Iain: British psychiatrist, doctor, and former Oxford literary scholar. Known particularly for his book *The Master and His Emissary*. 'The divided mind and the search for meaning' is a published essay that complements the longer volume. Quotation from his blog in *Psychology Today*, *The Skeptical Brain*. https://www.psychologytoday.com/us/blog/the-skeptical-brain/ 201012/the-curvilinearity-life.

Milne, A. A.: 1882–1956, English author. Words from *The House at Pooh Corner*.

Morgan, Henry: English spiritual director and author of *Approaches to Prayer* and *A Time to Reflect*. Quotation from his blog at http://www.annunciationtrust.org.uk/author/henry/.

Oliver, Mary: American poet. Words from *Our World*, her tribute to her deceased partner, Molly Malone Cook.

Paller, Ken and Voss, Joel L.: Professor of Psychology and Professor of Medical Social Sciences, Neurology and Psychiatry at Northwestern University USA. Information from 'An electrophysiological signature of unconscious recognition memory' published in *Nature Neuroscience*, 2009 https://www.ncbi.nlm.nih.gov/pmc/articles/PMC2692915/.

Parks, Tim: British author. Description from *Teach Us to Be Still*, p. 264.

Pert, Candace: 1946–2013, American neuroscientist and pharmacologist. Reference from her book *Molecules of Emotion*, p. 276.

Pullman, Philip: English novelist. Quote from an interview with Daniel Hahn at the Hay Festival: https://www.hayfestival.com/news/blog.aspx?post=416.

Reich, Wilhelm: 1897–1957, Austrian doctor of medicine and psychoanalyst. His work on 'body armour' influenced Gestalt and other therapies.

Rumi, Jalāl ad–Dīn Muhammad: 1207–1273, Persian poet and Sufi mystic. Prose quotation from his *Discourses* 53 in Coleman Barks' English version, *Essential Rumi*, p. 76. Some poetry quotations from translations by A. J. Arberry and Reynold A. Nicholson. Reference to Coleman Barks' version of 'Two Kinds of Intelligence'.

Scharmer, Otto: Senior Lecturer at MIT USA and Professor at Tsinghua University Beijing. Co-founder of the Presencing Institute.

Scott Peck, M: 1936–2005, American psychiatrist and author. Story from *The Road Less Traveled*.

Siegel, Dan: American clinical professor of psychology. Author of *The Developing Mind: How Relationships and the Brain Interact to Shape Who We Are* and *The Mindful Therapist*.

Sperry, Roger: 1913–1994, American neuropsychologist and neurobiologist. Won the Nobel prize for his work with split-brain research.

Sugawara, S.: Story of Japanese fisherman in 2011 tsunami recorded by CNN: http://edition.cnn.com/2011/WORLD/asiapcf/04/03/japan.tsunami.captain/index.html.

Tolle, Eckhart: Spiritual teacher and author of *The Power of Now* and *A New Earth*.

Thomas, R. S.: Welsh poet and Anglican priest. Quotation from his poem *The Bright Field*.

Turner, J. M. W.: 1775–1851, English Romantic artist. Reference from *Turner* by James Hamilton, quoted also at https://www.tate.org.uk/whats-on/tate-britain/display/romantics/romantics-room-guide-skying-looking-clouds.

Walter, Bruno: 1876–1962, German-born conductor who became a French citizen and settled in the USA. Described in Virginia Woolf's *Diaries*, p. 336.

Whyte, David: English poet. Words taken from his poem *Sweet Darkness*.

Woolf, Virginia: 1882–1941, English novelist. Quotes taken from her *Diaries*.

Yeats, W. B.: 1865–1939, Irish poet. Prose quotation from his book of folklore stories/essays, *The Celtic Twilight*. Also a line from his poem *Cloths of Heaven*.

INDEX